HOW TO WRITE BETTER DALL·E 3.0 PROMPTS BY EXAMPLE

By

Dr. Hesham Mohamed Elsherif

ABOUT THE AUTHOR

Dr. Hesham Mohamed Elsherif stands at the forefront of library management and research, boasting an impressive 22-year tenure in the field. Holding dual doctoral degrees, one in Management and Organizational Leadership and the other in Information Systems and Technology, Dr. Elsherif brings a unique blend of knowledge to any intellectual endeavor. An expert in Empirical research methodology, Dr. Elsherif specializes particularly in the Qualitative approach and Action research. This specialization has not only strengthened his research endeavors but has also allowed him to contribute invaluable insights and advancements in these areas.

Over the years, Dr. Elsherif has made significant contributions to the academic world not only as a professional researcher but also as an Adjunct Professor. This multifaceted role in the educational landscape has further solidified his reputation as a thought leader and pioneer. Furthermore, Dr. Elsherif's expertise isn't confined to one region. He has served as a consultant to numerous educational institutions on an international scale, sharing best practices, innovative strategies, and his deep insights into the ever-evolving realms of management and technology.

Combining a passion for education with an unparalleled depth of knowledge, Dr. Elsherif continues to inspire, educate, and lead in both the library and academic communities.

Dr. Hesham Mohamed Elsherif

PREFACE

In the ever-evolving landscape of artificial intelligence, the boundaries between technology and creativity are continuously being pushed. Among the most groundbreaking advancements is DALL·E 3.0, an AI model that transforms textual descriptions into vivid and imaginative images. This book, "How to Write Better DALL·E 3.0 Prompts," is dedicated to helping you harness the full potential of this remarkable tool by mastering the art of prompt writing.

The Power of Words

At its core, DALL·E 3.0 is a reflection of the prompts it receives. A well-crafted prompt can unlock the AI's potential to generate stunning visuals that are not only accurate but also deeply creative and engaging. Conversely, a vague or poorly structured prompt can lead to lackluster results. Therefore, understanding how to communicate effectively with DALL·E 3.0 is crucial for anyone looking to explore the frontiers of AI-generated art.

Bridging Technology and Creativity

This book serves as a comprehensive guide for both beginners and experienced users of DALL·E 3.0. Whether you are an artist seeking to expand your toolkit, a tech enthusiast curious about AI capabilities, or a professional looking to leverage AI in your work, this book provides the insights and techniques you need.

What to Expect

We begin with an introduction to DALL·E 3.0, exploring its features and capabilities, and how it differs from its predecessors. Understanding the technology behind DALL·E 3.0 will provide you with a solid foundation upon which to build your prompt-writing skills.

Next, we delve into the basics of prompt writing, covering the essential elements that make a prompt effective. We discuss the importance of clarity, specificity, and context, and how to avoid common pitfalls that can lead to ambiguous or unsatisfactory results.

From there, we move into more advanced techniques. You will learn how to infuse your prompts with emotions, leverage artistic styles, and use metaphors and symbolism to add depth and complexity to your images. We also explore various use cases, providing detailed examples that illustrate how different approaches can yield different results.

Optimizing and Troubleshooting

No process is without its challenges, and prompt writing is no exception. This book offers strategies for optimizing your prompts and troubleshooting common issues. By learning how to analyze and refine your prompts, you can continuously improve the quality of your generated images.

Ethical Considerations

As with any powerful technology, the use of DALL·E 3.0 comes with ethical responsibilities. We discuss the importance of using AI-generated art ethically, respecting copyright and intellectual property, and promoting inclusivity and diversity in your prompts. These considerations are crucial for ensuring that AI technology is used in a manner that benefits society as a whole.

Looking Ahead

Finally, we take a look at the future of AI art and prompt writing. Emerging trends and technologies promise to further expand the possibilities of what AI can achieve. By staying informed and adaptable, you can continue to be at the forefront of this exciting field.

A Journey of Exploration

Writing prompts for DALL·E 3.0 is as much an art as it is a science. It is a journey of exploration, experimentation, and discovery. This book is your companion on that journey, offering the knowledge and tools you need to unlock your creative potential and make the most of this extraordinary AI.

Thank you for embarking on this journey with us. We hope that "How to Write Better DALL·E 3.0 Prompts" will inspire you, challenge you, and ultimately help you create incredible AI-generated art that pushes the boundaries of imagination.

Happy prompting

Dr. Hesham Mohamed Elsherif

Table of Contents

Chapter 1: Understanding DALL·E 3.0 9

What is DALL·E 3.0? 9

Differences Between DALL·E 3.0 and Previous Versions 12

Key Features and Improvements 16

Chapter 2: Basics of Prompt Writing 21

What is a Prompt? 24

Anatomy Of a Good Prompt 28

Common Pitfalls to Avoid 33

Chapter 3: Crafting Effective Prompts 39

Clarity and Specificity 43

Context and Detail 46

Using Adjectives and Descriptors 51

Avoiding Ambiguity 54

Chapter 4: Advanced Prompt Techniques 59

Incorporating Emotions and Moods 62

Leveraging Styles and Artistic Movements 67

Using Metaphors and Symbolism 70

Experimenting With Creative Constraints 75

Chapter 5: Common Use Cases and Examples 80

Creating Realistic Images 84

Designing Fantastical and Surreal Scenes 89

Generating Character Designs 94

Developing Landscapes and Environments 99

Chapter 6: Prompt Optimization 105

Iterative Refinement 109

Analyzing Generated Outputs 113

Adjusting Prompts Based on Feedback 117

Chapter 7: Troubleshooting and Problem Solving 122

Addressing Common Issues 126

Handling Unexpected Results 131

Dealing With Limitations of DALL·E 3.0 136

Chapter 8: Ethics and Responsible Use 142

Ethical Considerations In AI-Generated Art 146

Respecting Copyright and Intellectual Property 150

Promoting Inclusivity and Diversity In Prompts 155

Chapter 9: Tools and Resources 162

Software And Platforms for Prompt Writing 168

Online Communities and Forums 174

Recommended Reading and Further Learning 179

Chapter 10: Future of AI Art and Prompt Writing 187

Emerging Trends and Technologies 192

Predictions For Future Developments 200

The Evolving Role of Prompt Writers 207

Example Prompts and Images 214

Complex Prompts and Images 220

APPENDICES 234

Glossary Of Terms 234

Sample Prompts and Outputs 239

Additional Resources and References 244

Chapter 1: Understanding DALL·E 3.0

What is DALL·E 3.0?

DALL·E 3.0 is a state-of-the-art AI model developed by OpenAI, designed to generate highly detailed and creative images from textual descriptions. The name "DALL·E" is a portmanteau of Salvador Dalí, the famous surrealist artist, and Pixar's WALL·E, reflecting the model's ability to blend artistic creativity with advanced technology. DALL·E 3.0 represents a significant leap forward in the field of artificial intelligence, building on the successes and lessons learned from its predecessors.

Key Features and Capabilities

Enhanced Creativity and Imagination:

DALL·E 3.0 excels in generating imaginative and highly creative images that push the boundaries of conventional art. It can create surreal scenes, fantastical creatures, and intricate designs that often surprise even the most seasoned artists and technologists.

Higher Resolution and Detail:

One of the standout features of DALL·E 3.0 is its ability to produce high-resolution images with exceptional detail. This capability allows for the creation of images that are not only visually stunning but also suitable for professional use in various fields such as marketing, entertainment, and design.

Improved Understanding of Context:

DALL·E 3.0 demonstrates a sophisticated understanding of context, enabling it to generate images that accurately reflect complex and nuanced prompts. It can interpret descriptive language, recognize relationships between objects, and maintain consistency in style and theme across multiple images.

Versatility in Styles and Genres:
This AI model is capable of producing images in a wide range of styles and genres. Whether you need a photorealistic rendering, a whimsical cartoon, or an abstract painting, DALL·E 3.0 can deliver. Its versatility makes it a powerful tool for artists, designers, and content creators looking to explore different visual approaches.

Integration of Artistic Movements:
DALL·E 3.0 can incorporate elements from various artistic movements and historical styles into its creations. By referencing specific periods or styles, users can generate images that evoke the essence of classical art, modernism, surrealism, and more.

How DALL·E 3.0 Works

DALL·E 3.0 is based on a deep learning architecture known as a transformer. This architecture allows the model to process and understand large amounts of data, making it particularly effective at generating coherent and contextually appropriate images from text descriptions. The model is trained on a diverse dataset that includes a wide range of images and corresponding textual descriptions. This extensive training enables DALL·E 3.0 to recognize patterns and relationships between words and visual elements, allowing it to generate images that accurately reflect the given prompts.

Text-to-Image Generation:
The core functionality of DALL·E 3.0 lies in its ability to translate textual descriptions into visual representations. When provided with a prompt, the model analyzes the text, identifies key elements, and synthesizes an image that embodies the described concepts. This process involves several steps, including understanding the semantics of the prompt, determining the appropriate visual style, and rendering the final image.

Iterative Refinement:

DALL·E 3.0 employs an iterative refinement process to enhance the quality and accuracy of its outputs. During this process, the model generates multiple versions of an image, each iteration improving upon the previous one. This approach ensures that the final image is as close to the user's vision as possible, with refined details and improved coherence.

Attention Mechanisms:

A critical component of DALL·E 3.0's architecture is its use of attention mechanisms. These mechanisms enable the model to focus on specific parts of the input text, allowing it to capture fine-grained details and complex relationships. By attending to different aspects of the prompt, DALL·E 3.0 can generate images that are not only visually appealing but also semantically accurate.

Applications of DALL·E 3.0

Art and Design:

DALL·E 3.0 is a valuable tool for artists and designers, offering endless possibilities for creative exploration. It can assist in brainstorming sessions, provide inspiration for new projects, and generate unique visual concepts that might not be achievable through traditional methods.

Marketing and Advertising:

In the marketing and advertising industries, DALL·E 3.0 can be used to create eye-catching visuals that capture the audience's attention. Its ability to produce high-quality images quickly and efficiently makes it an asset for developing compelling campaigns and promotional materials.

Entertainment and Media:

The entertainment and media sectors can benefit from DALL·E 3.0's capabilities in generating concept art, storyboards, and visual effects. Its ability to visualize fantastical elements and complex scenes makes it a valuable resource for filmmakers, game developers, and other creative professionals.

Education and Research:
DALL·E 3.0 also has applications in education and research, where it can be used to create visual aids, illustrate complex concepts, and enhance learning materials. Its ability to generate images from textual descriptions makes it a powerful tool for educators and researchers looking to convey information in a more engaging and accessible way.

The Future of DALL·E 3.0

As AI technology continues to advance, the potential applications of DALL·E 3.0 will expand even further. Future developments may include enhancements in image quality, greater control over visual styles, and improved integration with other AI systems. By staying at the forefront of AI research, DALL·E 3.0 and its successors will continue to revolutionize the way we create and interact with visual content.

In summary, DALL·E 3.0 represents a significant milestone in the field of AI-generated art. Its ability to transform textual descriptions into stunning images opens up new possibilities for creativity and innovation. Understanding how DALL·E 3.0 works and how to effectively communicate with it through well-crafted prompts is essential for anyone looking to harness its full potential.

Differences Between DALL·E 3.0 and Previous Versions

DALL·E 3.0 represents a significant evolution from its predecessors, bringing numerous enhancements and new features that improve its ability to generate high-quality images from textual descriptions. This section explores the key differences between DALL·E 3.0 and earlier versions, highlighting how these advancements contribute to its superior performance and broader capabilities.

Improved Image Quality and Resolution

Higher Resolution Outputs:

One of the most noticeable improvements in DALL·E 3.0 is the increased resolution of generated images. Earlier versions produced lower-resolution outputs that, while impressive, often lacked the fine details required for professional use. DALL·E 3.0, however, generates high-resolution images that are rich in detail and clarity. For instance, where DALL·E 1.0 might produce a basic outline of a complex scene, DALL·E 3.0 can render intricate textures, subtle lighting effects, and precise object details, making the images more visually appealing and realistic.

Example:

A prompt asking for "a bustling marketplace in a medieval town" in DALL·E 1.0 might result in a simplified depiction with basic shapes and colors. In contrast, DALL·E 3.0 can produce a detailed scene with cobblestone streets, individual market stalls filled with goods, and townspeople in period-appropriate clothing, all rendered with high resolution and intricate detail.

Enhanced Understanding of Context

Contextual Awareness:

DALL·E 3.0 has a much deeper understanding of context compared to its predecessors. Earlier versions sometimes struggled with complex prompts, leading to images that lacked coherence or failed to capture the intended scene accurately. DALL·E 3.0, however, excels in interpreting and maintaining contextual consistency across various elements of the prompt.

Example:

If given a prompt like "a futuristic city at sunset with flying cars and towering skyscrapers," DALL·E 2.0 might generate an image with some futuristic elements but miss the cohesiveness of the scene. DALL·E 3.0, on the other hand, can integrate all the elements seamlessly, ensuring that the sunset lighting affects the buildings and cars appropriately, creating a harmonious and believable scene.

Expanded Range of Styles and Genres

Versatility in Artistic Styles:
DALL·E 3.0 offers a broader range of artistic styles and genres, allowing users to specify not only the content of the image but also the desired artistic approach. Previous versions were somewhat limited in their stylistic flexibility, often defaulting to a generic visual style. DALL·E 3.0 can emulate various styles, from photorealism to abstract art, and everything in between.

Example:
A prompt such as "a portrait of a woman in the style of Vincent van Gogh" would yield vastly different results between versions. DALL·E 1.0 might produce a simple portrait with some abstract elements, while DALL·E 3.0 can create a detailed portrait featuring the characteristic brushstrokes and color palette of van Gogh, capturing the essence of his artistic style.

Better Handling of Complex and Abstract Concepts

Advanced Conceptualization:
DALL·E 3.0 is more adept at handling complex and abstract concepts than its predecessors. Earlier versions often produced literal interpretations of prompts, which could be limiting for more abstract or metaphorical descriptions. DALL·E 3.0, however, can generate images that reflect deeper, more nuanced understanding of abstract ideas.

Example:
A prompt like "the essence of happiness depicted as a surreal landscape" might have been challenging for DALL·E 1.0, resulting in a somewhat literal or confusing image. DALL·E 3.0, however, can produce a landscape filled with vibrant colors, joyful elements like balloons and sunshine, and whimsical features that capture the intangible feeling of happiness in a visually compelling way.

Improved Reliability and Consistency

Consistency in Outputs:
One of the challenges with earlier versions of DALL·E was the variability in the quality of outputs. DALL·E 3.0 introduces significant improvements in reliability and consistency, ensuring that the generated images meet a higher standard of quality more consistently. This improvement is particularly important for professional applications where consistent quality is essential.

Example:
For a prompt such as "a series of illustrations for a children's book featuring a young wizard," DALL·E 2.0 might produce some images that fit well together and others that seem out of place. DALL·E 3.0 can generate a cohesive series of illustrations that maintain consistent character design, color scheme, and style, making them suitable for use in a professional publication.

Enhanced User Control and Customization

Greater Customization Options:
DALL·E 3.0 provides users with more control over the image generation process, allowing for greater customization and refinement. This feature was less developed in earlier versions, which offered limited options for tweaking and refining the outputs.

Example:
If a user wants to generate "a sci-fi cityscape with specific architectural features and color schemes," DALL·E 2.0 might require multiple attempts to get the desired result. DALL·E 3.0, however, allows users to specify and adjust various parameters, such as the types of buildings, the overall color palette, and the atmospheric conditions, resulting in a more precise and tailored output.

The advancements in DALL·E 3.0 over its predecessors are substantial, making it a more powerful and versatile tool for generating high-quality, creative images from textual descriptions. With improved image quality, better contextual understanding, a wider range of styles, enhanced handling of complex concepts, greater reliability, and more user control, DALL·E 3.0 sets a new standard for AI-generated art. Understanding these differences is crucial for effectively leveraging the capabilities of DALL·E 3.0 and pushing the boundaries of what is possible in AI-driven creativity.

Key Features and Improvements

DALL·E 3.0 represents a significant advancement in AI technology, offering a range of features and improvements that enhance its ability to generate high-quality, imaginative images from textual descriptions. This section outlines the key features and improvements of DALL·E 3.0, illustrating how they contribute to its superior performance and versatility.

High-Resolution Image Generation

Enhanced Detail and Clarity:
DALL·E 3.0 is capable of producing high-resolution images with remarkable detail and clarity. This improvement allows for the

creation of images that are suitable for professional use, such as in marketing materials, publications, and digital art.

Example:
Consider a prompt like "a detailed illustration of a steampunk airship." In previous versions, the image might lack intricate details and appear somewhat simplistic. With DALL·E 3.0, the image will include fine details such as rivets on the metal panels, steam pipes, gears, and other mechanical components, all rendered with high clarity and precision.

Improved Contextual Understanding

Advanced Semantic Interpretation:
DALL·E 3.0 demonstrates a deep understanding of context, allowing it to generate images that accurately reflect complex and nuanced prompts. This feature ensures that the visual output aligns closely with the intended description.

Example:
For a prompt like "a futuristic cityscape at night with neon lights and flying cars," DALL·E 3.0 can accurately depict the nighttime setting with appropriate lighting effects, vibrant neon signs, and futuristic vehicles in motion, creating a coherent and immersive scene.

Versatile Artistic Styles

Diverse Style Emulation:
DALL·E 3.0 excels in emulating a wide range of artistic styles, from photorealism to abstract art. Users can specify the desired style, and the model will generate images that match the specified artistic approach.

Example:
A prompt such as "a portrait of a lion in the style of Picasso" would result in an image that captures the essence of Picasso's cubist

style, with geometric shapes, bold colors, and a unique interpretation of the lion's features.

Enhanced Creative Expression

Surreal and Imaginative Outputs:
DALL·E 3.0 is designed to handle creative and surreal prompts, producing imaginative and visually striking images. This capability allows for the exploration of artistic concepts that go beyond traditional representations.

Example:
For a prompt like "a dreamscape with floating islands, giant mushrooms, and a river of stars," DALL·E 3.0 can create a fantastical scene that vividly depicts the otherworldly elements described, blending them seamlessly into a cohesive and visually stunning image.

Detailed and Accurate Object Representation

Precision in Object Rendering:
DALL·E 3.0 can accurately represent objects with high precision, capturing intricate details and textures. This feature is particularly useful for generating images that require detailed and realistic depictions.

Example:
A prompt like "a close-up of a dragonfly's wings" will result in an image that shows the delicate structure of the wings, including the intricate patterns and translucent quality, rendered with exceptional detail and accuracy.

Enhanced User Control

Customization and Refinement:
DALL·E 3.0 offers greater control over the image generation process, allowing users to customize and refine their prompts. This

feature enables users to achieve more precise and tailored outputs, enhancing the overall creative experience.

Example:

If a user specifies a prompt like "a sunset over a tranquil lake with specific colors of the sky and water reflections," DALL·E 3.0 allows for adjustments to the color palette and reflection details, resulting in an image that matches the user's vision closely.

Improved Handling of Abstract Concepts

Abstract and Conceptual Visualization:

DALL·E 3.0 excels in visualizing abstract concepts, generating images that capture the essence of complex and non-literal ideas. This capability is valuable for artistic and conceptual projects.

Example:

A prompt such as "the concept of time depicted as a flowing river" would result in an image that metaphorically represents time with a flowing river, possibly incorporating elements like clocks, hourglasses, or other symbolic features to convey the abstract idea effectively.

Consistent Quality and Reliability

Reliable Output Quality:

DALL·E 3.0 ensures consistent quality in its generated images, reducing the variability seen in earlier versions. This reliability is crucial for professional applications where consistent and high-quality outputs are essential.

Example:

For a prompt like "a series of illustrations for a fantasy novel," DALL·E 3.0 can generate a cohesive set of images that maintain consistent character designs, settings, and artistic style, ensuring that the illustrations align well across the entire series.

Conclusion

DALL·E 3.0 brings a host of key features and improvements that make it a powerful and versatile tool for generating high-quality images from textual descriptions. With its enhanced resolution, improved contextual understanding, versatile artistic styles, and advanced creative capabilities, DALL·E 3.0 sets a new standard for AI-generated art. By leveraging these features, users can explore new realms of creativity and achieve stunning visual results that were previously unimaginable. Understanding these key features and improvements is essential for effectively utilizing DALL·E 3.0 and maximizing its potential in various creative and professional applications.

Chapter 2: Basics of Prompt Writing

Effective prompt writing is the cornerstone of creating high-quality images with DALL·E 3.0. A well-crafted prompt provides clear instructions to the AI, ensuring that the generated images align with your vision. This chapter covers the fundamental principles of prompt writing, offering practical examples to illustrate each concept.

Clarity and Specificity

Be Clear and Specific:

The more precise and detailed your prompt, the better DALL·E 3.0 can understand and generate the desired image. Ambiguity can lead to unexpected or inaccurate results.

Example:

Vague Prompt: "A forest scene."
Specific Prompt: "A dense forest with towering pine trees, a carpet of fallen leaves, and a narrow path winding through the trees at sunrise."

The specific prompt provides clear details about the type of forest, the elements within it, and the time of day, enabling DALL·E 3.0 to create a more accurate and visually rich image.

Context and Detail

Provide Contextual Information:

Including context helps DALL·E 3.0 understand the relationships between different elements in the scene.

Example:

Basic Prompt: "A woman reading a book."
Contextual Prompt: "A young woman with long brown hair, sitting

in a cozy armchair by the fireplace, reading a thick, leather-bound book on a rainy evening."

The contextual prompt not only describes the woman and the book but also sets the scene, providing details about the setting and atmosphere.

Using Adjectives and Descriptors

Incorporate Descriptive Language:
Adjectives and descriptive phrases add depth and richness to your prompts, helping DALL·E 3.0 capture the nuances of the scene.

Example:
Plain Prompt: "A mountain range."
Descriptive Prompt: "A majestic mountain range with snow-capped peaks, rugged cliffs, and lush green valleys, under a clear blue sky."

Descriptive language paints a vivid picture, allowing DALL·E 3.0 to generate an image that embodies the grandeur and beauty of the mountains.

Avoiding Ambiguity

Be Explicit to Avoid Misinterpretation:
Ambiguous prompts can lead to confusing or unintended results. Ensure that your descriptions are clear and unambiguous.

Example:
Ambiguous Prompt: "A cat on a mat."
Clear Prompt: "A fluffy white cat sitting on a colorful woven mat, next to a sunny window with a view of a garden."

The clear prompt specifies the appearance of the cat and the mat, as well as additional context about the setting, reducing the likelihood of misinterpretation.

Including Actions and Interactions

Describe Actions and Interactions:
If you want to depict movement or interactions between characters or objects, include these details in your prompt.

Example:
Static Prompt: "A dog and a boy."
Dynamic Prompt: "A playful golden retriever jumping to catch a frisbee thrown by a smiling boy in a park."

The dynamic prompt describes the action and interaction, creating a more engaging and lively scene.

Combining Multiple Elements

Integrate Multiple Elements Seamlessly:
When combining several elements, ensure that your prompt clearly describes how they fit together in the scene.

Example:
Separate Elements Prompt: "A boat, a lake, mountains."
Integrated Elements Prompt: "A small wooden boat floating on a serene lake, surrounded by towering mountains with snowy peaks, under a vibrant sunset sky."

The integrated prompt connects the elements cohesively, painting a complete and harmonious picture.

Specifying Styles and Mediums

Indicate Artistic Styles or Mediums:
If you have a specific artistic style or medium in mind, include this information in your prompt.

Example:
General Prompt: "A portrait of a woman."

Styled Prompt: "A portrait of a woman in the style of Renaissance oil painting, with detailed brushwork and a soft, glowing light."

Specifying the style guides DALL·E 3.0 in creating an image that aligns with your artistic vision.

Practical Exercises

Exercise 1:
Basic Prompt: "A garden."
Enhanced Prompt: "A vibrant flower garden with a variety of colorful blooms, a stone pathway, and a white picket fence, on a sunny spring day."

Exercise 2:
Basic Prompt: "A space scene."
Enhanced Prompt: "A futuristic space station orbiting a distant planet, with glowing nebulae and stars in the background, and small spacecraft docking at the station."

<u>What is a Prompt?</u>

A prompt is a concise and descriptive textual instruction provided to DALL·E 3.0, guiding the AI to generate an image based on the information given. The prompt serves as the foundation for the AI's creative process, encapsulating the user's vision and translating it into visual form. Understanding what constitutes an effective prompt is crucial for producing high-quality, accurate images.

The Role of a Prompt

Guiding the AI:
A prompt acts as a set of instructions for DALL·E 3.0, detailing what elements should be included in the image, how they should be arranged, and what overall style or mood the image should

convey. The better the prompt, the more likely the AI will generate an image that aligns with the user's expectations.

Example:
A simple prompt like "a sunset" provides minimal guidance, while a detailed prompt such as "a vivid sunset over a calm ocean with a sailboat in the foreground and seagulls flying in the sky" gives the AI a clearer idea of what the user wants to see.

Components of a Good Prompt

Clarity:
A prompt should be clear and easy to understand. Ambiguity can lead to unpredictable results, so it's important to be explicit about the details.

Example:
Unclear Prompt: "A scene with animals."
Clear Prompt: "A scene in a lush jungle with a family of elephants walking through the underbrush and colorful birds perched on the branches of tall trees."

Specificity:
Specific prompts yield more accurate and detailed images. Providing concrete details about the elements in the scene helps DALL·E 3.0 create a more precise representation.

Example:
General Prompt: "A mountain."
Specific Prompt: "A snow-capped mountain peak rising above a dense forest, with a clear blue sky and a river flowing at its base."

Context:
Including context helps the AI understand the relationships between different elements and how they should be depicted together.

Example:
Context-Lacking Prompt: "A house and a tree."
Contextual Prompt: "A cozy cottage with a thatched roof, nestled under a large oak tree, with a cobblestone path leading to the front door, in a rural countryside setting."

Descriptors:
Using descriptive language, such as adjectives and adverbs, adds depth and richness to the prompt, enhancing the final image.

Example:
Plain Prompt: "A car."
Descriptive Prompt: "A sleek, red sports car parked on a winding mountain road, with the sun setting in the background and the sky painted in shades of orange and pink."

Types of Prompts

Simple Prompts:
Simple prompts contain basic descriptions and are often used for generating straightforward images.

Example:
"An apple."

Detailed Prompts:
Detailed prompts include multiple elements and descriptions, providing a richer context for the AI to work with.

Example:
"A bright red apple with a shiny surface, resting on a wooden table next to an open book, with a window in the background showing a sunny garden."

Action-Oriented Prompts:
These prompts describe actions or interactions between elements in the scene, creating dynamic and engaging images.

Example:
"A young girl in a blue dress, blowing bubbles in a park, with a golden retriever playfully jumping to catch one."

Stylistic Prompts:
Stylistic prompts specify a particular artistic style or medium, guiding the AI to generate images in that aesthetic.

Example:
"A portrait of an old man with a long beard, in the style of a Renaissance oil painting, with soft, detailed brushstrokes and a warm color palette."

Crafting Effective Prompts

Be Explicit:
Clearly state what you want to see in the image. The more explicit the prompt, the less room there is for misinterpretation.

Example:
Implicit Prompt: "A garden scene."
Explicit Prompt: "A colorful flower garden with roses, tulips, and daisies, a stone path winding through it, and a wooden bench under a large oak tree."

Incorporate Key Details:
Include key details that are essential to the image you want. This helps the AI focus on the most important aspects.

Example:
Basic Prompt: "A cat on a chair."
Detailed Prompt: "A fluffy white cat curled up on a red velvet armchair, with a green blanket draped over the back and a fireplace in the background."

Use Relatable Comparisons:

Sometimes, comparing elements to familiar objects or scenes can help the AI understand your vision better.

Example:

"A futuristic city with skyscrapers that look like giant crystals, similar to the Emerald City in The Wizard of Oz, with flying cars zipping through the sky."

A prompt is more than just a simple description; it is the blueprint for the image that DALL·E 3.0 will create. By being clear, specific, contextual, and descriptive, you can effectively communicate your vision to the AI, resulting in high-quality, accurate, and visually appealing images. Mastering the basics of prompt writing is essential for leveraging the full potential of DALL·E 3.0 and achieving the best possible results.

<u>Anatomy Of a Good Prompt</u>

Creating an effective prompt for DALL·E 3.0 involves several key components that work together to guide the AI in generating the desired image. Understanding the anatomy of a good prompt will help you craft clear, specific, and detailed instructions that maximize the quality and accuracy of the resulting images.

1. Subject and Main Elements

Identify the Subject:

The subject is the primary focus of the image. Clearly stating the main subject ensures that the AI understands what the image is about.

Example:

Basic Subject: "A lighthouse."

Include Main Elements:
Along with the subject, include other important elements that should be present in the image. This helps create a complete and cohesive scene.

Example:
Main Elements Added: "A lighthouse on a rocky cliff, with waves crashing below and seagulls flying overhead."

2. Descriptive Adjectives

Enhance with Adjectives:
Adjectives add richness and detail to your prompt, helping DALL·E 3.0 visualize the specific characteristics of the elements in the scene.

Example:
Without Adjectives: "A house." *With Adjectives:* "A quaint, ivy-covered house with a red door and white shutters."

3. Context and Background

Provide Context:
Contextual information sets the scene and explains the relationships between the elements. This helps the AI place the subject and elements in a coherent setting.

Example:
Without Context: "A boy with a kite." *With Context:* "A boy with a colorful kite, running across a grassy field on a sunny day with a few fluffy clouds in the sky."

Background Details:
Adding background details enriches the scene, providing a fuller, more immersive image.

Example:
Background Added: "A boy with a colorful kite, running across a

grassy field on a sunny day, with a few fluffy clouds in the sky and a distant barn on the horizon."

4. Actions and Interactions

Describe Actions:
If the scene involves actions or interactions, clearly describe what is happening. This adds dynamism and life to the image.

Example:
Without Action: "A dog and a child." *With Action:* "A dog and a child playing fetch in a park, with the child throwing a ball and the dog eagerly chasing it."

Interactions:
Detailing interactions between elements makes the scene more engaging and realistic.

Example:
Interaction Added: "A dog and a child playing fetch in a park, with the child throwing a ball and the dog eagerly leaping to catch it mid-air."

5. Artistic Style and Medium

Specify the Style:
Indicate if you want the image in a particular artistic style or medium. This guides the AI in generating images that align with your artistic vision.

Example:
Without Style: "A portrait of a woman." *With Style:* "A portrait of a woman in the style of impressionist painting, with soft, blurred brushstrokes and a pastel color palette."

Medium Specifics:
Including the medium can further refine the output.

Example:
Medium Added: "A portrait of a woman in the style of impressionist painting, using oil on canvas, with soft, blurred brushstrokes and a pastel color palette."

6. Emotions and Moods

Convey Emotions:
Describing the emotions or mood you want to convey can help DALL·E 3.0 capture the intended atmosphere of the image.

Example:
Without Emotion: "A couple on a beach." *With Emotion:* "A couple on a beach at sunset, embracing and looking into each other's eyes, with a feeling of romance and tranquility."

Mood Details:
Elaborating on the mood can make the scene more evocative.

Example:
Mood Added: "A couple on a beach at sunset, embracing and looking into each other's eyes, with a feeling of romance and tranquility, as gentle waves lap at their feet and the sky is painted in shades of pink and orange."

7. Colors and Textures

Specify Colors:
Detailing colors adds vibrancy and specificity to the image, helping the AI capture the visual essence of the scene.

Example:
Without Colors: "A garden." *With Colors:* "A lush garden filled with vibrant flowers in shades of red, yellow, and purple, with a cobblestone path winding through it."

Describe Textures:
Including textures can enhance the tactile quality of the image.

Example:
Textures Added: "A lush garden filled with vibrant flowers in shades of red, yellow, and purple, with a cobblestone path winding through it and the rough texture of stone contrasting with the soft petals of the flowers."

Practical Examples

Example 1: Basic to Enhanced Prompt *Basic Prompt:* "A mountain lake." *Enhanced Prompt:* "A crystal-clear mountain lake surrounded by pine trees, with snow-capped peaks in the background, a wooden pier extending into the water, and a small cabin on the shore."

Example 2: Incorporating All Elements *Subject and Main Elements:* "A medieval castle." *Descriptive Adjectives:* "A grand, stone medieval castle." *Context and Background:* "A grand, stone medieval castle perched on a hilltop, overlooking a bustling village with thatched-roof cottages." *Actions and Interactions:* "A grand, stone medieval castle perched on a hilltop, overlooking a bustling village with thatched-roof cottages, with villagers going about their daily activities." *Artistic Style and Medium:* "A grand, stone medieval castle perched on a hilltop, overlooking a bustling village with thatched-roof cottages, with villagers going about their daily activities, in the style of a detailed historical illustration." *Emotions and Moods:* "A grand, stone medieval castle perched on a hilltop, overlooking a bustling village with thatched-roof cottages, with villagers going about their daily activities, in the style of a detailed historical illustration, evoking a sense of nostalgia and medieval charm." *Colors and Textures:* "A grand, stone medieval castle perched on a hilltop, overlooking a bustling village with thatched-roof cottages, with villagers going about their daily activities, in the style of a detailed historical illustration, evoking a sense of nostalgia and medieval charm, with the earthy tones of the stone castle contrasting with the vibrant colors of the village market stalls."

A good prompt is a well-crafted instruction that provides DALL·E 3.0 with the necessary details to generate high-quality, accurate images. By focusing on the subject and main elements, using descriptive adjectives, providing context and background, describing actions and interactions, specifying artistic styles and mediums, conveying emotions and moods, and detailing colors and textures, you can create prompts that effectively communicate your vision to the AI. Understanding the anatomy of a good prompt is essential for leveraging the full creative potential of DALL·E 3.0 and achieving the best possible results.

Common Pitfalls to Avoid

Crafting effective prompts for DALL·E 3.0 requires careful attention to detail and clarity. Even minor mistakes can lead to suboptimal or unintended results.

1. Vague Descriptions

Avoid Ambiguity:
Vague prompts can result in images that do not match your expectations. Be specific about what you want to see in the image.

Example:
Vague Prompt: "A tree."
Improved Prompt: "A tall oak tree with lush green leaves, standing in a grassy meadow under a clear blue sky."

Explanation:
The improved prompt specifies the type of tree, its environment, and additional details, making it easier for DALL·E 3.0 to generate an accurate image.

2. Overly Complex Prompts

Keep It Manageable:
While detail is important, overly complex prompts can confuse the AI. Break down complex scenes into simpler, manageable parts.

Example:
Complex Prompt: "A bustling city street with skyscrapers, people walking, cars driving, street vendors selling food, children playing, and birds flying, all at sunset."
Improved Prompt: "A bustling city street at sunset, with tall skyscrapers and people walking on the sidewalks."

Explanation:
The improved prompt focuses on key elements and simplifies the scene, making it easier for the AI to generate a coherent image. Additional details can be added in subsequent prompts if needed.

3. Lack of Context

Provide Context:
Without context, the AI might struggle to place elements correctly or create a coherent scene. Ensure your prompt includes enough context to guide the AI.

Example:
Lack of Context: "A dog and a tree."
Improved Prompt: "A golden retriever sitting under a large oak tree in a sunny park."

Explanation:
The improved prompt provides a setting and relationship between the elements, helping the AI create a more accurate and engaging image.

4. Inconsistent Details

Maintain Consistency:
Inconsistent details can confuse the AI and result in disjointed images. Ensure all parts of your prompt align with each other.

Example:
Inconsistent Prompt: "A modern cityscape with medieval knights on horseback."
Improved Prompt: "A modern cityscape with people walking and cars driving on the streets."

Explanation:
The improved prompt maintains consistency in the setting, ensuring that all elements fit together logically.

5. Overlooking Key Elements

Include Essential Details:
Omitting key elements can lead to incomplete or misleading images. Make sure your prompt includes all necessary components.

Example:
Overlooked Elements: "A beach scene."
Improved Prompt: "A beach scene with white sand, palm trees, and turquoise water, with a person lounging under an umbrella."

Explanation:
The improved prompt includes specific details that define the scene more clearly, ensuring a more accurate representation.

6. Redundancy and Repetition

Avoid Unnecessary Repetition:
Redundant or repetitive descriptions can waste space and confuse the AI. Be concise and to the point.

Example:
Redundant Prompt: "A beautiful, lovely, gorgeous sunset with an

amazing, stunning, incredible sky."
Improved Prompt: "A stunning sunset with vibrant colors in the sky."

Explanation:

The improved prompt eliminates redundancy, focusing on essential details to convey the desired image effectively.

7. Ignoring Artistic Style

Specify Style When Needed:

Failing to specify an artistic style can result in generic images. If a particular style is important, include it in your prompt.

Example:

No Style Specified: "A portrait of a woman."
Improved Prompt: "A portrait of a woman in the style of Renaissance painting, with detailed brushwork and warm tones."

Explanation:

The improved prompt specifies an artistic style, guiding the AI to produce an image that aligns with the desired aesthetic.

8. Missing Emotional Tone

Convey the Mood:

Ignoring the emotional tone can lead to images that lack the intended atmosphere. Use descriptive language to convey the mood.

Example:

No Emotional Tone: "A couple in a park."
Improved Prompt: "A couple in a park, holding hands and laughing, with the sun setting behind them, creating a warm and romantic atmosphere."

Explanation:

The improved prompt includes emotional context, helping the AI capture the intended mood and atmosphere.

Practical Examples of Avoiding Pitfalls

Example 1: Avoiding Vagueness and Adding Detail *Vague Prompt:* "A car on a road." *Improved Prompt:* "A red sports car driving on a winding mountain road, with a scenic view of the valley below."

Example 2: Simplifying Complex Scenes *Complex Prompt:* "A busy market with people shopping, vendors selling fruits and vegetables, children playing, musicians performing, and a parade in the background." *Improved Prompt:* "A busy market with vendors selling fruits and vegetables and people shopping."

Example 3: Ensuring Consistent Details *Inconsistent Prompt:* "An astronaut riding a horse in the ocean." *Improved Prompt:* "An astronaut floating in space near a space station, with Earth visible in the background."

Avoiding common pitfalls is essential for crafting effective prompts that yield high-quality images with DALL·E 3.0. By being specific, providing context, maintaining consistency, including key elements, avoiding redundancy, specifying artistic styles, and conveying emotional tones, you can create prompts that guide the AI more accurately and efficiently. Understanding these pitfalls and how to avoid them will enhance your ability to communicate your vision clearly, resulting in better and more satisfying AI-generated images.

Conclusion

Mastering the basics of prompt writing is essential for creating high-quality images with DALL·E 3.0. By being clear and specific, providing context and detail, using descriptive language, avoiding ambiguity, describing actions and interactions, integrating multiple elements, and specifying styles and mediums, you can effectively communicate your vision to the AI. These principles, combined with practice and experimentation, will help you unlock the full creative potential of DALL·E 3.0.

Chapter 3: Crafting Effective Prompts

Crafting effective prompts is crucial for achieving high-quality and accurate images with DALL·E 3.0. A well-crafted prompt provides clear, detailed instructions that guide the AI in generating the desired image.

1. Clarity and Specificity

Be Clear and Specific:
Effective prompts are clear and specific, leaving no room for ambiguity. The more detailed and precise your prompt, the better the AI can understand and generate the intended image.

Example:
General Prompt: "A forest."
Specific Prompt: "A dense forest with towering pine trees, a carpet of fallen leaves, and a narrow path winding through the trees at sunrise."

The specific prompt provides clear details about the type of forest, the elements within it, and the time of day, helping the AI create a more accurate image.

2. Context and Detail

Provide Context:
Context helps the AI understand the relationships between different elements in the scene. Including background information and setting details can make your prompts more effective.

Example:
Context-Lacking Prompt: "A girl with a book."
Contextual Prompt: "A young girl with long brown hair, sitting on a cozy armchair by the fireplace, reading a thick, leather-bound book on a rainy evening."

The contextual prompt not only describes the girl and the book but also sets the scene, providing details about the setting and atmosphere.

3. Descriptive Adjectives

Use Descriptive Adjectives:
Incorporating adjectives and descriptive phrases adds depth and richness to your prompts, enhancing the final image.

Example:
Plain Prompt: "A mountain range."
Descriptive Prompt: "A majestic mountain range with snow-capped peaks, rugged cliffs, and lush green valleys, under a clear blue sky."

Descriptive language paints a vivid picture, allowing the AI to generate an image that embodies the grandeur and beauty of the mountains.

4. Actions and Interactions

Describe Actions and Interactions:
If your scene involves movement or interactions between characters or objects, clearly describe these actions. This adds dynamism and life to the image.

Example:
Static Prompt: "A dog and a boy."
Dynamic Prompt: "A playful golden retriever jumping to catch a frisbee thrown by a smiling boy in a park."

The dynamic prompt describes the action and interaction, creating a more engaging and lively scene.

5. Combining Multiple Elements

Integrate Multiple Elements Seamlessly:
When combining several elements, ensure that your prompt clearly describes how they fit together in the scene.

Example:
Separate Elements Prompt: "A boat, a lake, mountains."
Integrated Elements Prompt: "A small wooden boat floating on a serene lake, surrounded by towering mountains with snowy peaks, under a vibrant sunset sky."

The integrated prompt connects the elements cohesively, painting a complete and harmonious picture.

6. Artistic Style and Medium

Specify Artistic Styles or Mediums:
If you have a specific artistic style or medium in mind, include this information in your prompt to guide the AI's creative process.

Example:
General Prompt: "A portrait of a woman."
Styled Prompt: "A portrait of a woman in the style of Renaissance oil painting, with detailed brushwork and a soft, glowing light."

Specifying the style guides the AI in creating an image that aligns with your artistic vision.

7. Emotions and Moods

Convey Emotions and Moods:
Describing the emotions or mood you want to convey can help the AI capture the intended atmosphere of the image.

Example:
No Emotion: "A couple on a beach."
Emotional Prompt: "A couple on a beach at sunset, embracing and looking into each other's eyes, with a feeling of romance and tranquility."

The emotional prompt includes emotional context, helping the AI capture the intended mood and atmosphere.

8. Colors and Textures

Specify Colors and Textures:
Detailing colors and textures adds vibrancy and specificity to the image, helping the AI capture the visual essence of the scene.

Example:
Without Colors: "A garden."
With Colors and Textures: "A lush garden filled with vibrant flowers in shades of red, yellow, and purple, with a cobblestone path winding through it and a wooden bench under a blooming cherry tree."

The detailed prompt includes specific colors and textures, enhancing the visual richness of the generated image.

Practical Examples

Example 1: From Basic to Detailed Prompt *Basic Prompt:* "A cityscape."
Detailed Prompt: "A bustling cityscape at dusk, with skyscrapers illuminated by glowing lights, cars moving on the streets, and people walking on the sidewalks, with a clear view of the river reflecting the city lights."

Example 2: Creating a Complex Scene *Basic Elements:* "A castle, a dragon, a knight."
Integrated Prompt: "A grand medieval castle perched on a hilltop, with a fierce dragon flying above it, breathing fire, while a brave knight in shining armor stands at the castle gates, ready to defend."

Example 3: Specifying Artistic Style and Emotion *Basic Prompt:* "A landscape."
Styled and Emotional Prompt: "A serene landscape in the style of a

Japanese ink painting, with a calm river flowing through a valley surrounded by cherry blossom trees in full bloom, evoking a sense of peace and tranquility."

Clarity and Specificity

Clarity and specificity are fundamental to crafting effective prompts for DALL·E 3.0. Clear and specific prompts provide detailed guidance to the AI, ensuring that the generated images closely match your vision. This section delves into the importance of clarity and specificity, offering practical examples to illustrate these principles.

Importance of Clarity

Avoiding Ambiguity:
Ambiguous prompts can lead to unpredictable or unsatisfactory results. Being clear about what you want ensures that DALL·E 3.0 understands your instructions and produces an image that meets your expectations.

Example:
Ambiguous Prompt: "A man in a park."
Clear Prompt: "A middle-aged man wearing a blue jacket and jeans, sitting on a wooden bench in a park, feeding pigeons."

The clear prompt provides specific details about the man's appearance, clothing, and actions, as well as the setting, reducing ambiguity and guiding the AI more effectively.

Importance of Specificity

Providing Detailed Descriptions:
Specificity involves including detailed descriptions of the elements in your prompt. This helps the AI generate images with the desired features and characteristics.

Example:
General Prompt: "A car."
Specific Prompt: "A vintage red convertible with white leather seats, parked in front of a retro diner with neon lights at night."

The specific prompt includes details about the car's type, color, and interior, as well as the setting, leading to a more accurate and visually interesting image.

Combining Clarity and Specificity

Creating Comprehensive Prompts:
Combining clarity and specificity results in comprehensive prompts that leave little room for misinterpretation. This approach ensures that the AI has all the information it needs to generate high-quality images.

Example:
Basic Prompt: "A mountain."
Comprehensive Prompt: "A snow-capped mountain peak rising above a dense pine forest, with a crystal-clear lake reflecting the mountain and a hiker in the foreground looking up at the peak."

The comprehensive prompt provides a detailed description of the mountain, surrounding environment, and an additional element (the hiker), creating a rich and coherent scene.

Practical Techniques for Clarity and Specificity

Use Clear Language:
Avoid vague or ambiguous terms. Use precise language to describe what you want.

Example:
Vague: "A nice house."
Clear: "A cozy, two-story house with a red brick facade, white trim, and a neatly manicured lawn."

Include Specific Details:

Incorporate specific details about the elements in your prompt. Describe their characteristics, colors, and positions.

Example:

General: "A tree by a river."

Specific: "A tall willow tree with drooping branches, standing on the bank of a gently flowing river, with ducks swimming near the shore."

Break Down Complex Scenes:

For complex scenes, break down the elements into manageable parts and describe each part clearly.

Example:

Complex: "A busy market."

Broken Down: "A bustling market square with colorful stalls selling fruits and vegetables, people shopping, a street musician playing a guitar, and a fountain in the center."

Specify Actions and Interactions:

If the scene involves actions or interactions, describe them clearly to guide the AI.

Example:

General: "A child with a balloon."

Specific: "A young girl in a yellow dress holding a red balloon, skipping down a cobblestone path in a park, with trees and flowers on either side."

Use Relatable Comparisons:

Comparing elements to familiar objects or scenes can help the AI understand your vision better.

Example:

"An alien landscape with rock formations resembling giant

mushrooms, under a sky filled with swirling, colorful clouds like a Van Gogh painting."

Examples of Clarity and Specificity

Example 1: Simple to Detailed *Simple Prompt:* "A cat."
Detailed Prompt: "A fluffy white Persian cat with blue eyes, sitting on a windowsill with sunlight streaming in, looking out at a garden."

Example 2: Enhancing Context *Basic Prompt:* "A street at night."
Enhanced Prompt: "A quiet cobblestone street at night, illuminated by vintage street lamps, with ivy-covered brick buildings on either side and a full moon in the sky."

Example 3: Specifying Artistic Style and Elements *Basic Prompt:* "A portrait."
Specific Prompt: "A portrait of an elderly woman with a warm smile, wearing a colorful headscarf, painted in the style of a classical oil painting with rich, textured brushstrokes."

Clarity and specificity are essential for crafting effective prompts that yield high-quality images with DALL·E 3.0. By using clear language, including specific details, breaking down complex scenes, specifying actions and interactions, and using relatable comparisons, you can create prompts that effectively communicate your vision to the AI. Mastering these principles will enhance your ability to generate accurate and visually appealing images, unlocking the full creative potential of DALL·E 3.0.

Context and Detail

In the realm of crafting effective prompts for DALL·E 3.0, context and detail are pivotal. These elements help the AI understand the scene's setting, relationships between objects, and the specific characteristics of each component.

Importance of Context

Setting the Scene:
Context establishes the setting of the image, providing background information that helps the AI generate a coherent and accurate depiction. It places the subject within a broader environment, giving the image depth and meaning.

Example:
Without Context: "A horse."
With Context: "A majestic brown horse standing in a sunlit meadow, surrounded by wildflowers, with a backdrop of rolling hills and a clear blue sky."

In the context-rich prompt, the horse is situated within a specific environment, making the image more complete and visually appealing.

Establishing Relationships:
Context also helps define the relationships between different elements in the scene, ensuring they fit together logically.

Example:
Without Context: "A dog and a cat."
With Context: "A playful golden retriever and a curious tabby cat sitting together on a cozy living room rug, in front of a crackling fireplace."

The context explains how the dog and cat are interacting and their surroundings, creating a more coherent image.

Importance of Detail

Enhancing Specificity:
Detailed descriptions provide clear, specific information about

each element in the scene, guiding the AI to generate precise and accurate images.

Example:
Basic Detail: "A tree."
Enhanced Detail: "A towering oak tree with broad, green leaves and a sturdy trunk, with a wooden swing hanging from one of its lower branches."

The detailed prompt gives specific characteristics of the tree, resulting in a more vivid and accurate depiction.

Adding Depth and Texture:
Details add depth and texture to the image, making it richer and more engaging.

Example:
Basic Detail: "A mountain."
Enhanced Detail: "A snow-capped mountain peak with jagged cliffs, surrounded by dense pine forests, with a crystal-clear lake at its base reflecting the early morning sunlight."

The enhanced detail describes the mountain's features and surroundings, creating a more textured and lifelike image.

Combining Context and Detail

Creating Comprehensive Prompts:
Combining context and detail results in comprehensive prompts that provide all the necessary information for the AI to generate high-quality images.

Example:
Basic Prompt: "A beach."
Comprehensive Prompt: "A serene beach with golden sand, gentle waves lapping at the shore, and tall palm trees swaying in the

breeze. A colorful beach umbrella and a towel are set up near the water, with a family playing in the background."

The comprehensive prompt includes contextual information and detailed descriptions, creating a complete and engaging scene.

Practical Techniques for Context and Detail

Use Specific Descriptions:
Avoid vague terms. Use specific descriptions to provide clear, detailed information.

Example:
Vague: "A bird."
Specific: "A bright red cardinal perched on a snow-covered pine branch, with its feathers fluffed up against the cold."

Incorporate Background Elements:
Include background elements to provide context and make the scene more immersive.

Example:
Without Background: "A castle."
With Background: "A grand medieval castle perched on a rocky hill, overlooking a bustling village with thatched-roof cottages and cobblestone streets."

Describe Actions and Interactions:
Specify actions and interactions to add dynamism and clarity to the scene.

Example:
Without Action: "A child with a kite."
With Action: "A young boy running through a grassy field, flying a colorful kite high in the sky, with a gentle breeze blowing."

Detail the Environment:
Provide details about the environment to enhance the context and depth of the image.

Example:
Basic Environment: "A garden."
Detailed Environment: "A lush garden filled with blooming roses, tulips, and daisies, with a cobblestone path winding through it and a wooden bench under a blossoming cherry tree."

Examples of Context and Detail

Example 1: Simple to Detailed *Simple Prompt:* "A park."
Detailed Prompt: "A quiet park with green lawns, tall oak trees providing shade, a small pond with ducks swimming, and a white gazebo in the center, surrounded by blooming flowers."

Example 2: Adding Background and Detail *Basic Prompt:* "A city street."
Contextual and Detailed Prompt: "A bustling city street at dusk, with people walking on the sidewalks, yellow taxis honking in traffic, neon signs illuminating the buildings, and a street musician playing a violin near a subway entrance."

Example 3: Combining Context and Detail for a Complete Scene *Basic Prompt:* "A market."
Comprehensive Prompt: "A lively market square filled with colorful stalls selling fresh fruits, vegetables, and flowers. Shoppers browse the goods, while a street vendor prepares delicious snacks at a food cart. Children play near a fountain in the center, and the smell of baked bread wafts through the air."

Context and detail are crucial for crafting effective prompts that yield high-quality images with DALL·E 3.0. By providing a clear setting, establishing relationships between elements, and offering specific descriptions, you can guide the AI to create accurate, engaging, and visually rich images. Mastering the use of context and detail will enhance your ability to communicate your vision clearly, unlocking the full potential of DALL·E 3.0.

Using Adjectives and Descriptors

Adjectives and descriptors are essential tools in crafting effective prompts for DALL·E 3.0. They add depth, clarity, and vividness to your descriptions, helping the AI generate more accurate and visually appealing images.

Importance of Adjectives and Descriptors

Adding Detail and Specificity:

Adjectives and descriptors provide specific details about the elements in your prompt. This helps the AI understand exactly what characteristics you want in the generated image.

Example:

Without Adjectives: "A cat."
With Adjectives: "A fluffy white cat with bright blue eyes, sitting on a red velvet cushion."

The use of adjectives adds detail, making the image more specific and vivid.

Enhancing Visual Imagery:

Adjectives and descriptors create richer visual imagery by conveying textures, colors, shapes, and other sensory details.

Example:

Without Adjectives: "A tree."
With Adjectives: "A tall oak tree with rough bark and vibrant green leaves, standing in a sunlit meadow."

The adjectives help paint a clearer picture, making it easier for the AI to generate an accurate image.

Conveying Emotions and Moods:

Adjectives and descriptors can also convey emotions and moods, adding an extra layer of meaning to the image.

Example:

Without Adjectives: "A beach."
With Adjectives: "A tranquil beach with soft white sand and gentle waves, under a warm, golden sunset."

The adjectives create a serene and peaceful mood, guiding the AI to generate an image that captures this atmosphere.

Practical Techniques for Using Adjectives and Descriptors

Be Specific and Precise:

Choose adjectives that precisely convey the characteristics you want to emphasize. Avoid vague or general terms.

Example:

Vague: "A nice house."
Specific: "A charming, two-story Victorian house with a wraparound porch, painted in pastel blue and white."

Use Sensory Descriptions:

Incorporate sensory details to make your descriptions more vivid and engaging. Think about how things look, feel, sound, smell, or taste.

Example:

Basic: "A flower."
Sensory: "A delicate pink rose with velvety petals and a sweet, fragrant aroma."

Combine Multiple Adjectives:

Using multiple adjectives can provide a fuller description and add richness to your prompt. Just be sure they complement each other and enhance the overall image.

Example:
Single Adjective: "A car."
Multiple Adjectives: "A sleek, red sports car with a shiny finish and black leather seats."

Use Comparisons and Metaphors:
Comparisons and metaphors can make your descriptions more relatable and vivid by linking unfamiliar elements to familiar ones.

Example:
"A towering skyscraper with windows that shimmer like a million tiny mirrors."

Incorporate Emotional and Atmospheric Descriptors:
Describe the emotions and atmosphere you want to convey in the scene to guide the AI's interpretation.

Example:
Without Emotion: "A city at night."
With Emotion: "A bustling city at night, with streets glowing from neon signs, casting a vibrant, electric energy."

Examples of Using Adjectives and Descriptors

Example 1: Simple to Enhanced *Simple:* "A garden."
Enhanced: "A lush, green garden filled with blooming roses, tulips, and daisies, with a stone pathway winding through it and a wooden bench under a blossoming cherry tree."

Example 2: Adding Sensory Details *Basic:* "A fireplace."
Sensory: "A cozy stone fireplace crackling with warm, amber flames, the smell of burning pine filling the room, and soft, flickering light casting shadows on the walls."

Example 3: Combining Multiple Adjectives *Single Adjective:* "A mountain."
Multiple Adjectives: "A majestic, snow-capped mountain with

rugged cliffs and a dense forest at its base, bathed in the golden light of dawn."

Example 4: Using Comparisons and Metaphors *Basic:* "A lake."
With Comparison: "A serene lake with water as smooth as glass, reflecting the surrounding pine trees like a mirror."

Example 5: Incorporating Emotional and Atmospheric Descriptors *Without Emotion:* "A forest."
With Emotion: "A mysterious, ancient forest shrouded in mist, with towering trees and an eerie, quiet atmosphere."

Using adjectives and descriptors effectively is crucial for crafting prompts that yield high-quality images with DALL·E 3.0. By being specific and precise, incorporating sensory details, combining multiple adjectives, using comparisons and metaphors, and describing emotions and atmosphere, you can create rich, detailed prompts that guide the AI to generate accurate and visually stunning images. Mastering the use of adjectives and descriptors will enhance your ability to communicate your vision clearly, unlocking the full potential of DALL·E 3.0.

Avoiding Ambiguity

Avoiding ambiguity in prompt writing is essential for generating high-quality and accurate images with DALL·E 3.0. Ambiguous prompts can lead to unclear, misleading, or unintended results.

Importance of Avoiding Ambiguity

Ensuring Accuracy:
Clear and unambiguous prompts help ensure that DALL·E 3.0 accurately interprets your instructions and generates the desired image.

Example:
Ambiguous Prompt: "A man with a dog."
Clear Prompt: "A young man with short brown hair, wearing a blue jacket, walking a golden retriever on a leash in a park."

The clear prompt provides specific details about the man and the dog, as well as the context, reducing ambiguity.

Reducing Misinterpretation:
Ambiguous prompts can lead to multiple interpretations, resulting in images that do not match your expectations. Being precise helps reduce the chances of misinterpretation.

Example:
Ambiguous Prompt: "A child by a tree."
Clear Prompt: "A young girl with curly blonde hair, wearing a red dress, sitting under a large oak tree, reading a book."

The clear prompt specifies the child's appearance, actions, and the type of tree, making the scene more precise.

Practical Techniques for Avoiding Ambiguity

Be Specific About Key Elements:
Clearly describe the key elements of the scene, including their characteristics, actions, and relationships.

Example:
Ambiguous: "A boat on a lake."
Specific: "A small wooden rowboat with a red stripe, floating on a calm blue lake, surrounded by tall pine trees."

Include Contextual Information:
Providing context helps DALL·E 3.0 understand how elements fit together in the scene.

Example:
Ambiguous: "A woman and a cat."

Contextual: "A woman with long black hair, wearing a green dress, sitting on a sofa with a fluffy white cat curled up on her lap, in a cozy living room."

Avoid Vague Descriptions:
Use precise language to describe elements, avoiding vague terms that could lead to multiple interpretations.

Example:
Ambiguous: "A car by a building."
Clear: "A vintage red convertible parked in front of a retro diner with neon signs, at night."

Specify Actions and Interactions:
Describe actions and interactions between elements to create a clear and dynamic scene.

Example:
Ambiguous: "A man and a dog in a garden."
Specific: "A man in a straw hat, kneeling in a vegetable garden, planting seeds, while a small brown dog digs a hole nearby."

Use Relatable Comparisons:
Comparisons can help clarify your descriptions by linking unfamiliar elements to familiar ones.

Example:
"A towering skyscraper with windows that shimmer like a thousand diamonds in the sunlight."

Avoid Overly Complex Prompts:
While detail is important, overly complex prompts can confuse the AI. Break down complex scenes into simpler parts if necessary.

Example:
Complex: "A busy street with people shopping, cars driving, street vendors selling food, children playing, and musicians performing."

Simpler: "A busy street with people shopping and street vendors selling food."

Examples of Avoiding Ambiguity

Example 1: From Ambiguous to Clear *Ambiguous Prompt:* "A bird on a branch."
Clear Prompt: "A bright red cardinal perched on a snow-covered pine branch, with the forest in the background."

Example 2: Adding Context and Detail *Ambiguous Prompt:* "A house in a field."
Contextual and Detailed Prompt: "A quaint, white cottage with a thatched roof, surrounded by a field of yellow sunflowers, under a clear blue sky."

Example 3: Describing Actions and Interactions *Ambiguous Prompt:* "A boy and a dog."
Specific Prompt: "A young boy with curly brown hair, wearing a blue t-shirt and jeans, running through a park while a golden retriever chases after him, both laughing and barking."

Example 4: Using Relatable Comparisons *Ambiguous Prompt:* "A tall building."
Clear Prompt: "A sleek, modern skyscraper with glass walls reflecting the sunset, standing tall like a shimmering beacon in the city skyline."

Avoiding ambiguity is crucial for crafting effective prompts that yield high-quality and accurate images with DALL·E 3.0. By being specific about key elements, including contextual information, avoiding vague descriptions, specifying actions and interactions, using relatable comparisons, and simplifying complex scenes, you can create clear and precise prompts that guide the AI more effectively. Mastering the art of avoiding ambiguity will enhance your ability to communicate your vision clearly, resulting in better and more satisfying AI-generated images.

Conclusion

Crafting effective prompts for DALL·E 3.0 involves clarity, specificity, context, descriptive language, dynamic actions, cohesive element integration, artistic styles, emotional tones, and detailed colors and textures. By focusing on these principles, you can create prompts that effectively communicate your vision to the AI, resulting in high-quality, accurate, and visually appealing images. Mastering the art of prompt writing is essential for unlocking the full creative potential of DALL·E 3.0 and achieving the best possible results

Chapter 4: Advanced Prompt Techniques

Once you have mastered the basics of crafting clear and specific prompts, you can explore advanced techniques to further refine your prompts and achieve more creative and nuanced results with DALL·E 3.0.

Incorporating Emotions and Moods

Convey Emotional Tone:

Describing the desired emotional tone of the image helps DALL·E 3.0 capture the atmosphere and mood you want to convey.

Example:

Neutral Prompt: "A forest."
Emotional Prompt: "A tranquil forest bathed in the soft golden light of dawn, with a sense of peaceful stillness."

Creating Atmosphere:

Including details that evoke a specific atmosphere can make the scene more immersive and emotionally resonant.

Example:

Neutral Prompt: "A beach at sunset."
Atmospheric Prompt: "A serene beach at sunset, with waves gently lapping at the shore and the sky painted in shades of pink and orange, creating a romantic and calming ambiance."

Leveraging Artistic Styles

Specify Art Styles:

Indicating a particular art style can guide the AI to generate images that align with specific aesthetic preferences.

Example:

Without Style: "A portrait of a woman."

With Style: "A portrait of a woman in the style of Art Nouveau, with flowing lines, intricate patterns, and a pastel color palette."

Combining Styles:
You can also combine multiple styles to create unique and interesting visuals.

Example:
"An urban cityscape in the style of cyberpunk and Impressionism, with neon lights and soft, blurred brushstrokes."

Using Metaphors and Symbolism

Incorporate Symbolic Elements:
Using metaphors and symbolism can add depth and layers of meaning to your prompts, resulting in more thought-provoking images.

Example:
Literal Prompt: "A clock."
Symbolic Prompt: "A weathered clock with melting hands, symbolizing the fluid and fleeting nature of time."

Metaphorical Descriptions:
Describing elements metaphorically can create more evocative and imaginative scenes.

Example:
"A dragon soaring above the clouds, its scales shimmering like molten gold in the sunlight, representing power and majesty."

Experimenting with Creative Constraints

Impose Creative Constraints:
Setting creative constraints can lead to more innovative and unexpected results by challenging the AI to work within specific boundaries.

Example:
Without Constraint: "A landscape."
With Constraint: "A monochromatic landscape with varying shades of blue, featuring a river winding through a snow-covered valley."

Use Contradictory Elements:
Combining contradictory elements can produce intriguing and surreal images.

Example:
"A futuristic city with ancient ruins interspersed among sleek, modern skyscrapers, blending past and future."

Examples of Advanced Prompt Techniques

Example 1: Emotional and Atmospheric *Basic Prompt:* "A mountain."
Advanced Prompt: "A majestic mountain peak shrouded in mist, with a sense of mystery and awe as the first light of dawn breaks through the clouds."

Example 2: Artistic Styles *Basic Prompt:* "A garden."
Advanced Prompt: "A vibrant garden depicted in the style of Van Gogh, with swirling brushstrokes and bold, vivid colors."

Example 3: Metaphors and Symbolism *Basic Prompt:* "A bird in a cage."
Advanced Prompt: "A delicate songbird in a gilded cage, with the door slightly ajar, symbolizing the tension between freedom and confinement."

Example 4: Creative Constraints *Basic Prompt:* "A street scene."
Advanced Prompt: "A bustling street scene rendered entirely in black and white, except for a single red umbrella held by a passerby."

Practical Tips for Advanced Prompt Techniques

Combine Techniques:
Don't hesitate to combine multiple advanced techniques in a single prompt to create even richer and more complex images.

Example:
"A serene forest clearing at twilight, painted in the style of Japanese ink wash, with fireflies glowing softly among the trees, evoking a sense of magical tranquility."

Iterative Refinement:
Use iterative refinement to gradually enhance your prompts. Start with a basic description and add layers of detail, style, and emotional tone through multiple iterations.

Example:

1. "A cat on a windowsill."

2. "A black cat on a windowsill, with sunlight streaming in."

3. "A sleek black cat lounging on a sunlit windowsill, with warm golden light creating a peaceful atmosphere."

Challenge the AI:
Push the boundaries of what DALL·E 3.0 can do by experimenting with unusual or complex prompts. This can lead to surprising and creative outcomes.

Example:
"A steampunk airship floating above a futuristic city, with gears and cogs visible in the ship's hull, blending Victorian and sci-fi elements."

<u>Incorporating Emotions and Moods</u>

Incorporating emotions and moods into your prompts can significantly enhance the depth and resonance of the images generated by DALL·E 3.0. By clearly communicating the emotional tone and atmosphere you want to convey, you can guide the AI to create images that evoke specific feelings and experiences.

Why Incorporate Emotions and Moods?

Creating Emotional Impact:

Images that convey a clear emotional tone can be more engaging and impactful. They resonate more deeply with viewers, making the visual experience more memorable.

Example:

Neutral Prompt: "A child in a garden."
Emotional Prompt: "A joyful child laughing and playing in a sunlit garden filled with blooming flowers."

The emotional prompt creates a vivid, happy scene that is more likely to evoke a positive emotional response.

Enhancing Atmosphere:

Describing the mood of a scene helps DALL·E 3.0 understand the broader context and generate images that capture the desired atmosphere.

Example:

Neutral Prompt: "A forest at night."
Atmospheric Prompt: "A mysterious forest at night, with a pale moon casting eerie shadows through the twisted branches."

The atmospheric prompt sets a specific mood, enhancing the visual and emotional impact of the image.

Techniques for Incorporating Emotions and Moods

Use Descriptive Language:

Incorporate adjectives and adverbs that convey the desired

emotional tone. Words like "serene," "joyful," "melancholic," and "intense" can help set the mood.

Example:
Neutral Prompt: "A sunset over the ocean."
Emotional Prompt: "A breathtaking sunset over the ocean, with the sky ablaze in vibrant hues of orange and pink, creating a sense of wonder and awe."

Create Contextual Scenarios:
Describe scenarios or actions that naturally evoke certain emotions. Including interactions and dynamic elements can make the scene more emotionally engaging.

Example:
Neutral Prompt: "A couple in a park."
Emotional Prompt: "A couple in a park, holding hands and laughing as they walk along a flower-lined path, with a gentle breeze rustling the leaves."

Highlight Sensory Details:
Sensory details can intensify the emotional experience by engaging multiple senses. Describe how things look, feel, sound, or even smell.

Example:
Neutral Prompt: "A winter scene."
Sensory and Emotional Prompt: "A peaceful winter scene with softly falling snowflakes, the crisp air tingling with the scent of pine, and the muffled sounds of a distant stream flowing under a blanket of snow."

Incorporate Symbolic Elements:
Use symbols and metaphors to add layers of meaning and evoke specific emotions. Symbolic elements can convey complex emotional states effectively.

Example:

Neutral Prompt: "A lonely person on a bench."

Symbolic Prompt: "A solitary figure sitting on a weathered park bench, surrounded by fallen autumn leaves, under a gray, overcast sky, symbolizing solitude and reflection."

Examples of Incorporating Emotions and Moods

Example 1: Joyful and Uplifting *Neutral Prompt:* "A girl with a balloon."

Emotional Prompt: "A cheerful girl with a bright red balloon, skipping along a sun-dappled path in a vibrant meadow, her laughter echoing in the air."

Example 2: Calm and Serene *Neutral Prompt:* "A lake at sunrise."

Emotional Prompt: "A tranquil lake at sunrise, with the water reflecting the soft pastel colors of the dawn sky, and a gentle mist rising from the surface, creating a sense of peace and serenity."

Example 3: Sad and Reflective *Neutral Prompt:* "A rainy city street."

Emotional Prompt: "A melancholic city street in the rain, with glistening cobblestones reflecting the dim streetlights, and a lone figure walking with an umbrella, evoking a sense of solitude and reflection."

Example 4: Exciting and Adventurous *Neutral Prompt:* "A mountain climber."

Emotional Prompt: "A daring mountain climber scaling a rugged peak, with the wind whipping through their hair and a determined look on their face, capturing the thrill and intensity of the climb."

Practical Tips for Incorporating Emotions and Moods

Visualize the Scene:

Before writing your prompt, take a moment to visualize the scene and consider what emotions you want it to evoke. This can help you choose the right words to describe it.

Example:
Imagine a peaceful, early morning in a small village. How does it feel? Quiet, calm, hopeful? Use these feelings to guide your prompt.

Use Metaphors and Similes:
Metaphors and similes can add depth and emotion to your descriptions by comparing elements to familiar emotional experiences.

Example:
"A sunset as brilliant as a painter's masterpiece, casting a warm, golden glow over the landscape."

Be Consistent:
Ensure that all elements of your prompt support the intended emotion or mood. Inconsistencies can dilute the emotional impact.

Example:
Inconsistent Prompt: "A peaceful garden with a roaring bonfire."
Consistent Prompt: "A peaceful garden with a small, crackling firepit, surrounded by blooming flowers and the soft chirping of crickets."

Incorporating emotions and moods into your prompts is an advanced technique that can greatly enhance the quality and impact of the images generated by DALL·E 3.0. By using descriptive language, creating contextual scenarios, highlighting sensory details, and incorporating symbolic elements, you can guide the AI to produce images that evoke specific emotions and create a rich, immersive experience. Mastering this technique will allow you to harness the full creative potential of DALL·E 3.0, resulting in more expressive and emotionally resonant images.

<u>Leveraging Styles and Artistic Movements</u>

Leveraging styles and artistic movements in your prompts can help DALL·E 3.0 generate images that align with specific aesthetic preferences and historical art traditions. By specifying the desired style or movement, you can guide the AI to create visually unique and culturally rich images.

Why Leverage Styles and Artistic Movements?

Achieving Aesthetic Precision:

Specifying an artistic style or movement helps ensure that the generated images reflect particular visual qualities, such as color schemes, brushwork, and composition, making the images more tailored to your needs.

Example:

A generic prompt might yield an image that is too broad or stylistically inconsistent.
A style-specific prompt like "A portrait in the style of Renaissance oil painting" will yield a more precise and consistent aesthetic.

Evoking Historical and Cultural Contexts:

Incorporating historical and cultural contexts through specific styles and movements can add depth and meaning to your images, making them more resonant and engaging.

Example:

A generic prompt for a landscape might lack cultural significance.
A prompt like "A Japanese garden in the style of traditional ukiyo-e" evokes cultural and historical richness.

Techniques for Leveraging Styles and Artistic Movements

Specify Art Styles:
Clearly mention the desired art style to guide the AI in adopting the characteristic features of that style.

Example:
Without Style: "A cityscape."
With Style: "A cityscape in the style of Impressionism, with soft, blurred brushstrokes and vibrant colors."

Incorporate Artistic Movements:
Refer to specific artistic movements to capture the broader visual and thematic elements associated with those movements.

Example:
"An abstract composition inspired by Cubism, with geometric shapes and fragmented forms."

Combine Multiple Styles:
Blend elements from different styles and movements to create unique and innovative visuals.

Example:
"A futuristic cityscape combining elements of Art Deco and Cyberpunk, with sleek, geometric architecture and neon lights."

Use Descriptive Language Aligned with Styles:
Use adjectives and descriptors that are commonly associated with the chosen style or movement to reinforce the desired aesthetic.

Example:
Without Descriptive Alignment: "A forest."
With Descriptive Alignment: "A mystical forest depicted in the style of Surrealism, with dreamlike, fantastical elements and unusual color contrasts."

Examples of Leveraging Styles and Artistic Movements

Example 1: Classical Art Styles *Basic Prompt:* "A portrait of a woman."
Style-Specific Prompt: "A portrait of a woman in the style of Renaissance oil painting, with detailed brushwork, realistic proportions, and a warm, glowing light."

Example 2: Modern Art Movements *Basic Prompt:* "A landscape."
Movement-Specific Prompt: "A landscape in the style of Impressionism, with loose, fluid brushstrokes, capturing the play of light and color in a vibrant, natural scene."

Example 3: Blending Styles *Basic Prompt:* "A street scene."
Blended Style Prompt: "A lively street scene blending elements of Pop Art and Graffiti, with bold, vibrant colors, dynamic compositions, and street art influences."

Example 4: Cultural Art Movements *Basic Prompt:* "A festival."
Movement-Specific Prompt: "A lively festival scene depicted in the style of traditional Mexican folk art, with bright, vivid colors, intricate patterns, and a festive atmosphere."

Practical Tips for Leveraging Styles and Artistic Movements

Research and Reference:
Familiarize yourself with different art styles and movements to better understand their characteristics and how to describe them in your prompts.

Example:
"Research the key features of Art Nouveau, such as flowing lines, organic forms, and intricate details, to effectively incorporate them into your prompt."

Be Consistent:
Ensure that all elements of your prompt are consistent with the chosen style or movement to create a cohesive image.

Example:
Inconsistent Prompt: "A medieval castle in the style of Baroque, with modern skyscrapers in the background."
Consistent Prompt: "A medieval castle in the style of Gothic architecture, with intricate stone carvings and pointed arches."

Experiment with Fusion:
Don't be afraid to experiment by fusing different styles and movements to create novel and visually interesting images.

Example:
"A whimsical landscape combining elements of Surrealism and Impressionism, with dreamlike scenes painted in vibrant, loose brushstrokes."

Use Style-Related Vocabulary:
Incorporate vocabulary related to the chosen style or movement to enhance the specificity and richness of your prompts.

Example:
"An Art Deco poster design featuring sleek, geometric shapes, bold lines, and luxurious, metallic colors."

Leveraging styles and artistic movements in your prompts allows you to guide DALL·E 3.0 to generate images that are aesthetically precise and culturally rich. By specifying art styles, incorporating artistic movements, blending styles, and using descriptive language aligned with those styles, you can create visually unique and engaging images. Mastering these techniques will enhance your ability to produce AI-generated art that is not only accurate but also rich in artistic expression and historical context.

<u>**Using Metaphors and Symbolism**</u>

Incorporating metaphors and symbolism into your prompts can add depth, layers of meaning, and artistic richness to the images generated by DALL·E 3.0. These techniques allow you to convey complex ideas and emotions in a visually compelling way.

Why Use Metaphors and Symbolism?

Enhancing Visual Storytelling:
Metaphors and symbolism can transform simple images into powerful visual stories, making them more engaging and thought-provoking.

Example:
A literal prompt might describe a sunset, while a symbolic prompt might use a sunset to represent the end of an era.

Adding Depth and Complexity:
Using metaphors and symbolism introduces layers of meaning, encouraging viewers to look beyond the surface and explore deeper interpretations.

Example:
A tree can symbolize growth, strength, or family, depending on the context provided in the prompt.

Techniques for Using Metaphors and Symbolism

Identify Key Concepts:
Start by identifying the key concepts or themes you want to convey. Think about the abstract ideas or emotions you want to represent visually.

Example:
If you want to convey the idea of freedom, you might use images of open skies, birds in flight, or unchained objects.

Use Symbolic Imagery:
Incorporate objects, scenes, or actions that are commonly associated with the abstract concepts you wish to depict.

Example:
Freedom: "A soaring eagle above a vast, open landscape." *Time:* "An ancient clock with melting hands, symbolizing the fluidity of time."

Employ Metaphorical Descriptions:
Use metaphors to draw parallels between the visual elements and the abstract ideas they represent.

Example:
Metaphorical Prompt: "A lighthouse standing tall amidst a stormy sea, symbolizing guidance and hope in times of trouble."

Create Visual Analogies:
Visual analogies can effectively communicate complex ideas by comparing them to more familiar or tangible objects.

Example:
"An old, twisted tree with deep roots and sprawling branches, symbolizing a person's journey through life with experiences and growth."

Examples of Using Metaphors and Symbolism

Example 1: Personal Growth *Literal Prompt:* "A young plant." *Metaphorical Prompt:* "A young plant breaking through the soil, symbolizing new beginnings and personal growth."

Example 2: Resilience *Literal Prompt:* "A mountain." *Symbolic Prompt:* "A lone mountain standing tall against the force of the wind, symbolizing resilience and strength."

Example 3: Change and Transformation *Literal Prompt:* "A butterfly." *Metaphorical Prompt:* "A butterfly emerging from its chrysalis, symbolizing change and transformation."

Example 4: Inner Peace *Literal Prompt:* "A calm lake." *Symbolic Prompt:* "A calm lake at dawn, with its surface reflecting the sky like a mirror, symbolizing inner peace and tranquility."

Practical Tips for Using Metaphors and Symbolism

Choose Universally Recognizable Symbols:
Opt for symbols that are widely understood and carry universal meanings to ensure your message is clear.

Example:
An anchor can symbolize stability, while a dove often represents peace.

Combine Multiple Symbols:
Using multiple symbols in a single prompt can enrich the image and convey more complex ideas.

Example:
"A phoenix rising from ashes under a sky filled with storm clouds, symbolizing rebirth and resilience amid adversity."

Use Context to Clarify Symbolism:
Provide context to help DALL·E 3.0 understand the intended symbolism and generate an image that accurately reflects your vision.

Example:
"A candle flickering in the dark, representing a glimmer of hope in times of despair."

Balance Literal and Symbolic Elements:
Combine literal descriptions with symbolic elements to create images that are both visually appealing and rich in meaning.

Example:
"A solitary figure walking along a deserted beach at sunset, with footprints in the sand symbolizing the journey of life."

Examples of Combined Literal and Symbolic Prompts

Example 1: Hope and Perseverance *Literal Elements:* "A climber reaching the summit of a mountain." *Symbolic Elements:* "A climber reaching the summit of a mountain, with rays of sunlight breaking through the clouds, symbolizing hope and perseverance."

Example 2: Isolation and Introspection *Literal Elements:* "A person sitting on a bench in a park." *Symbolic Elements:* "A person sitting on a bench in a park, surrounded by fallen leaves, with the bench placed at the edge of a misty lake, symbolizing isolation and introspection."

Example 3: Wisdom and Time *Literal Elements:* "An old man reading a book." *Symbolic Elements:* "An old man reading a book under the shade of an ancient oak tree, with fallen leaves around him, symbolizing wisdom and the passage of time."

Using metaphors and symbolism in your prompts allows you to convey complex ideas and emotions through visually compelling imagery. By identifying key concepts, incorporating symbolic imagery, employing metaphorical descriptions, and creating visual analogies, you can guide DALL·E 3.0 to generate images that are rich in meaning and artistic depth. Mastering these techniques will enhance your ability to produce AI-generated art that resonates on a deeper level, evoking powerful emotional and intellectual responses.

Experimenting With Creative Constraints

Experimenting with creative constraints can lead to innovative and unexpected results when generating images with DALL·E 3.0. By setting specific limitations or rules for the AI, you can challenge it to explore new directions and produce unique visual outputs.

Why Use Creative Constraints?

Fostering Innovation:
Constraints can push the boundaries of creativity by forcing the AI to think outside the box. This can result in novel and surprising images that might not be produced under typical conditions.

Example:
Without Constraint: "A flower in a garden."
With Constraint: "A flower in a garden, rendered entirely in shades of blue."

Enhancing Focus:
Constraints help narrow down the focus of the prompt, making it easier to achieve specific aesthetic or thematic goals.

Example:
Without Constraint: "A busy street scene."
With Constraint: "A busy street scene depicted using only geometric shapes."

Techniques for Experimenting with Creative Constraints

Color Constraints:
Limit the color palette to create a distinctive visual style or mood. This can also emphasize certain aspects of the image.

Example:
Full Color: "A mountain landscape."

Color Constraint: "A mountain landscape depicted in monochromatic tones of green."

Temporal Constraints:
Specify a particular time period or historical context to influence the style and elements of the image.

Example:
Modern Context: "A cityscape."
Temporal Constraint: "A cityscape as it might appear in the 1920s, with Art Deco architecture and vintage cars."

Stylistic Constraints:
Restrict the image to a particular artistic style or medium, guiding the AI to adhere to specific visual conventions.

Example:
Without Style: "A portrait of a woman."
Stylistic Constraint: "A portrait of a woman in the style of pointillism, composed entirely of tiny dots."

Form and Composition Constraints:
Define specific compositional rules or forms, such as symmetry, minimalism, or abstraction, to shape the overall structure of the image.

Example:
Without Composition Constraint: "A beach scene."
Form Constraint: "A minimalist beach scene with only essential elements depicted using simple shapes and lines."

Thematic Constraints:
Focus on a specific theme or concept, limiting the elements in the scene to those that align with the chosen theme.

Example:
General Theme: "A celebration."

Thematic Constraint: "A celebration inspired by nature, with all decorations and elements made from natural materials like flowers, leaves, and wood."

Examples of Experimenting with Creative Constraints

Example 1: Monochromatic Color Palette *Without Constraint:* "A bustling marketplace." *With Constraint:* "A bustling marketplace depicted entirely in shades of sepia, creating a vintage look."

Example 2: Historical Context *Without Constraint:* "A family dinner." *With Constraint:* "A family dinner as it might appear in the Victorian era, with period-appropriate attire and decor."

Example 3: Artistic Style *Without Constraint:* "A landscape." *With Constraint:* "A landscape painted in the style of Cubism, with fragmented shapes and abstract forms."

Example 4: Minimalism *Without Constraint:* "A living room." *With Constraint:* "A minimalist living room with only a few essential pieces of furniture, clean lines, and a neutral color palette."

Example 5: Nature-Themed Celebration *Without Constraint:* "A birthday party." *With Constraint:* "A birthday party set in a forest, with decorations made from leaves, flowers, and wooden elements."

Practical Tips for Experimenting with Creative Constraints

Start with a Clear Concept:
Begin with a clear idea of what you want to achieve and then define the constraints that will guide the AI in generating the image.

Example:
Concept: "A futuristic city." Constraint: "Depicted using only black and white, with a high contrast, noir-style aesthetic."

Combine Multiple Constraints:
Combining different types of constraints can lead to even more unique and interesting results.

Example:
"A portrait of a musician, depicted in the style of Cubism, using only shades of blue and green, with an emphasis on geometric shapes."

Iterate and Refine:
Experiment with different constraints and refine your prompts based on the results. Iterative refinement can help you achieve the desired outcome.

Example:
Initial Prompt: "A garden in autumn, depicted using only warm colors." Refined Prompt: "A garden in autumn, with vibrant orange and red leaves, and golden sunlight filtering through the trees, using only warm colors."

Balance Creativity and Clarity:
While constraints foster creativity, ensure that your prompt remains clear and specific to guide the AI effectively.

Example:
Unclear Constraint: "An abstract scene." *Clear Constraint:* "An abstract cityscape with skyscrapers and streets, depicted using only triangular shapes."

Experimenting with creative constraints is an advanced technique that can unlock new levels of innovation and artistic expression when generating images with DALL·E 3.0. By setting color, temporal, stylistic, form, and thematic constraints, you can challenge the AI to explore different visual directions and produce unique and compelling results. Mastering the use of creative constraints will enhance your ability to generate AI art that is not only visually striking but also conceptually rich and distinctive.

Conclusion

Advanced prompt techniques enable you to achieve more creative, nuanced, and visually striking results with DALL·E 3.0. By incorporating emotions and moods, leveraging artistic styles, using metaphors and symbolism, and experimenting with creative constraints, you can guide the AI to generate images that are not only accurate but also rich in meaning and aesthetic appeal. Mastering these advanced techniques will enhance your ability to explore the full potential of AI-generated art and create truly unique and captivating images.

Chapter 5: Common Use Cases and Examples

DALL·E 3.0 is a powerful AI tool capable of generating a wide range of images from textual descriptions. Its versatility makes it suitable for various applications across different fields.

1. Realistic Images

Creating Realistic Scenes:
DALL·E 3.0 excels at generating highly detailed and realistic images based on specific prompts. This capability is useful for creating visual content that closely resembles real-life scenarios.

Example:
Prompt: "A bustling New York City street in the rain, with people holding umbrellas, yellow taxis driving by, and reflections on the wet pavement."

The generated image will capture the vibrancy and realism of a rainy day in New York City, with detailed reflections and atmospheric elements.

Product Visualization:
Businesses can use DALL·E 3.0 to visualize products in various settings, helping in marketing and advertising efforts.

Example:
Prompt: "A modern living room with a sleek, white sofa, a glass coffee table, and a large window overlooking a city skyline."

The image can be used in promotional materials to showcase the product in a realistic and appealing environment.

2. Fantastical and Surreal Images

Creating Imaginary Worlds:
DALL·E 3.0 can generate fantastical and surreal images that go

beyond the limitations of reality. This is particularly useful for creative projects such as book covers, game design, and concept art.

Example:
Prompt: "A floating island in the sky with a cascading waterfall, lush greenery, and mythical creatures like dragons and unicorns."

The image will depict an enchanting, otherworldly scene that captures the imagination.

Surreal Art:
Artists can use DALL·E 3.0 to explore surreal concepts and create visually striking artwork.

Example:
Prompt: "A melting clock hanging from a tree branch in a desert, with a surreal, dreamlike quality inspired by Salvador Dalí."

The generated image will have a surrealistic style, reminiscent of Dalí's famous works.

3. Character Design

Creating Unique Characters:
DALL·E 3.0 can help designers and storytellers create unique characters with specific attributes and appearances.

Example:
Prompt: "A brave knight with silver armor, a blue cape, and a glowing sword, standing in a medieval castle."

The image will depict a detailed and visually appealing character suitable for use in stories, games, or animations.

Costume and Fashion Design:
Fashion designers can visualize new clothing designs and styles.

Example:
Prompt: "A futuristic outfit with metallic fabrics, LED lights, and sleek, geometric patterns, worn by a model on a runway."

The image can serve as a visual prototype for new fashion concepts.

4. Landscape and Environment Design

Designing Natural Landscapes:
DALL·E 3.0 can generate beautiful and diverse natural landscapes for use in environmental design, tourism, and media.

Example:
Prompt: "A serene mountain landscape at sunrise, with snow-capped peaks, a clear blue lake, and a dense pine forest."

The image will capture the beauty and tranquility of a natural landscape.

Urban and Architectural Visualization:
Urban planners and architects can visualize urban spaces and architectural designs.

Example:
Prompt: "A modern urban park with green spaces, walking paths, a playground, and a central fountain surrounded by skyscrapers."

The image can be used to illustrate the proposed design of an urban space.

5. Educational and Scientific Illustrations

Educational Diagrams and Illustrations:
DALL·E 3.0 can create detailed and accurate illustrations for educational materials, making complex concepts easier to understand.

Example:
Prompt: "A detailed cross-section of a volcano, showing the magma chamber, vents, and lava flow during an eruption."

The image can be used in textbooks or educational presentations to explain volcanic activity.

Scientific Visualization:
Scientists can visualize abstract scientific concepts and data.

Example:
Prompt: "A visual representation of the solar system, with the sun at the center and the planets orbiting around it, each labeled with their names."

The image can help illustrate scientific concepts in a clear and engaging manner.

6. Marketing and Advertising

Creating Engaging Visuals:
Marketers can use DALL·E 3.0 to create eye-catching visuals for advertising campaigns and social media content.

Example:
Prompt: "A vibrant advertisement for a tropical vacation, featuring a pristine beach, turquoise waters, and a luxury resort."

The image can attract attention and promote the advertised destination effectively.

Product Advertisements:
Businesses can visualize products in creative and appealing ways.

Example:
Prompt: "A stylish coffee maker on a kitchen counter, with freshly brewed coffee, coffee beans, and a morning sunlight streaming through the window."

The image can be used in advertisements to highlight the product's appeal.

<u>Creating Realistic Images</u>

One of the most powerful applications of DALL·E 3.0 is its ability to generate highly detailed and realistic images based on textual descriptions. This capability is invaluable across various fields, including marketing, product visualization, media, and more.

Marketing and Advertising

Product Visualization:
DALL·E 3.0 can create lifelike images of products, making them more appealing to potential customers. This is particularly useful for marketing materials and online advertisements.

Example:
Prompt: "A sleek, modern smartphone with a glass back, placed on a wooden table next to a cup of coffee and a laptop, with natural light streaming in from a nearby window."

The generated image will showcase the smartphone in a realistic and attractive setting, highlighting its design and features.

Lifestyle Marketing:
Brands can create lifestyle images that show their products in use, helping to connect with the target audience on an emotional level.

Example:
Prompt: "A family enjoying a barbecue in their backyard, with a modern gas grill, colorful plates of food, and children playing on the grass under a clear blue sky."

The image will capture a lively and inviting scene, promoting the product within a relatable context.

Product Design and Prototyping

Design Prototypes:
DALL·E 3.0 can visualize design concepts and prototypes, aiding in the product development process. This helps designers and engineers see potential products in realistic settings before manufacturing.

Example:
Prompt: "A new model of an electric car parked in a modern city street, with sleek lines, aerodynamic design, and a charging station nearby."

The image will provide a realistic representation of the car in an urban environment, useful for design reviews and presentations.

Packaging Design:
Brands can visualize their product packaging to see how it might look on store shelves or in customers' hands.

Example:
Prompt: "A high-end skincare product in an elegant, minimalist bottle, placed on a marble countertop in a well-lit bathroom."

The image will help evaluate the packaging design's aesthetic appeal and practicality.

Media and Content Creation

Editorial Illustrations:
Journalists and content creators can use DALL·E 3.0 to generate realistic images for articles, blog posts, and other media, enhancing the visual appeal and engagement of their content.

Example:
Prompt: "A busy newsroom with journalists working on computers, stacks of papers on desks, and a large screen displaying breaking news headlines."

The image will illustrate the dynamic environment of a newsroom, adding visual context to a written piece about journalism.

Book Covers and Illustrations:
Authors and publishers can create realistic book covers and illustrations that accurately represent the content of their books.

Example:
Prompt: "A historical novel set in Victorian London, featuring a detailed street scene with horse-drawn carriages, cobblestone roads, and people in period clothing."

The image will provide an authentic visual representation of the book's setting, attracting potential readers.

Architectural Visualization

Real Estate Marketing:
DALL·E 3.0 can generate realistic images of properties, helping real estate agents market homes more effectively.

Example:
Prompt: "A luxurious beachfront villa with large glass windows, a private pool, and a beautiful sunset over the ocean."

The image will highlight the villa's features and scenic location, appealing to potential buyers.

Interior Design:
Interior designers can visualize their design concepts in realistic settings, aiding in client presentations and decision-making.

Example:
Prompt: "A modern living room with a white sectional sofa, a glass coffee table, abstract art on the walls, and a floor-to-ceiling window with a city view."

The image will provide a detailed look at the proposed design, helping clients envision the final result.

Scientific and Educational Visualizations

Educational Illustrations:

Educators can use DALL·E 3.0 to create realistic illustrations that make complex concepts easier to understand.

Example:

Prompt: "A detailed cross-section of the human heart, showing the chambers, valves, and blood flow pathways."

The image will serve as a valuable educational tool, helping students grasp the anatomy and function of the heart.

Scientific Visualizations:

Scientists can generate realistic images to visualize data, phenomena, or theoretical models.

Example:

Prompt: "A realistic depiction of a black hole in space, with a swirling accretion disk and light bending around the event horizon."

The image will aid in explaining complex astrophysical concepts to a broader audience.

Practical Tips for Creating Realistic Images

Be Specific:

Include as many details as possible in your prompt to ensure the generated image is accurate and realistic.

Example:

Basic Prompt: "A kitchen." *Detailed Prompt:* "A modern kitchen with white cabinets, a stainless steel refrigerator, a marble island with bar stools, and pendant lights hanging from the ceiling."

Use Descriptive Language:
Employ descriptive adjectives and phrases to add depth and clarity to your prompts.

Example:
Basic Prompt: "A park." *Descriptive Prompt:* "A lush, green park with tall oak trees, a winding gravel path, a wooden bench, and a playground with children playing."

Incorporate Context:
Provide context to help DALL·E 3.0 understand the setting and relationships between elements.

Example:
Basic Prompt: "A person reading." *Contextual Prompt:* "A young woman with glasses sitting on a cozy armchair by the fireplace, reading a hardcover book, with a cat curled up on her lap."

Iterate and Refine:
Experiment with different prompts and refine them based on the generated results to achieve the desired level of realism.

Example:
Initial Prompt: "A cozy bedroom." Refined Prompt: "A cozy bedroom with a queen-sized bed, fluffy pillows and a comforter, a nightstand with a lamp, and a window with sheer curtains letting in soft morning light."

Creating realistic images with DALL·E 3.0 involves using specific, descriptive, and contextual prompts to guide the AI effectively. By leveraging its capabilities, you can generate high-quality visuals for marketing, product design, media, architecture, education, and science. Mastering the art of crafting detailed and precise prompts will enable you to produce realistic images that meet your specific needs and enhance your projects.

Designing Fantastical and Surreal Scenes

DALL·E 3.0 is exceptionally well-suited for creating fantastical and surreal scenes that push the boundaries of imagination. This capability is particularly valuable in fields such as art, entertainment, gaming, and storytelling, where vivid and unconventional visuals are often needed.

Art and Creative Projects

Surreal Artworks:
Artists can use DALL·E 3.0 to generate surreal artworks that defy reality and create visually stunning pieces.

Example:
Prompt: "A dreamlike landscape with floating islands connected by golden bridges, with cascading waterfalls that flow upwards into the sky."

The image will depict a fantastical scene that challenges conventional perceptions of gravity and space, ideal for surreal art exhibitions.

Conceptual Art:
DALL·E 3.0 can help artists visualize abstract concepts and ideas in unique and imaginative ways.

Example:
Prompt: "A giant clock with melting numbers draped over a tree branch in a barren desert, symbolizing the fluidity of time."

The image will provide a powerful visual metaphor that can be used in conceptual art pieces.

Entertainment and Media

Book Covers and Illustrations:
Authors and publishers can create captivating book covers and illustrations that reflect the fantastical elements of their stories.

Example:
Prompt: "A mystical forest with glowing mushrooms, towering ancient trees with faces, and ethereal wisps of light floating through the air."

The image will capture the enchanting and otherworldly atmosphere of a fantasy novel, attracting potential readers.

Movie and Game Concept Art:
Filmmakers and game developers can visualize scenes and settings for their projects, helping to establish the tone and style of their worlds.

Example:
Prompt: "A cyberpunk city with neon-lit streets, hovering vehicles, and humanoid robots interacting with humans."

The image will provide a detailed and visually rich concept for a futuristic and surreal urban environment.

Gaming and Interactive Media

Game Environments:
Game designers can use DALL·E 3.0 to create immersive and imaginative game environments that enhance the player experience.

Example:
Prompt: "An underwater city with bioluminescent buildings, colorful coral reefs, and diverse marine life swimming around."

The image will depict a vibrant and fantastical underwater world, perfect for an adventure game setting.

Character Design:
Designing unique and surreal characters that fit within fantastical worlds.

Example:
Prompt: "A humanoid creature with butterfly wings, glowing eyes, and an iridescent skin that changes color with its emotions."

The image will provide a detailed and imaginative character design for a fantasy game or story.

Storytelling and World-Building

Creating Unique Worlds:
Writers and world-builders can visualize the unique settings and cultures of their fictional worlds, aiding in the creative process.

Example:
Prompt: "A floating city made of crystal, with airships docking at skyports and streets made of light that change color with the time of day."

The image will help flesh out the details of a unique and fantastical world, making it more vivid and coherent.

Mythical Creatures and Beings:
Designing mythical creatures and beings that inhabit fantastical worlds.

Example:
Prompt: "A majestic dragon with scales that shimmer like gold, wings that sparkle with stars, and eyes that glow with an inner fire."

The image will bring to life a powerful and awe-inspiring mythical creature.

Advertising and Marketing

Creative Campaigns:
Brands can use fantastical and surreal imagery in advertising campaigns to capture attention and create memorable impressions.

Example:
Prompt: "A whimsical tea party in a floating garden, with teapots pouring tea by themselves and pastries that levitate."

The image will create a magical and engaging visual, perfect for marketing a unique product or event.

Product Promotion:
Using surreal visuals to promote products in a creative and eye-catching manner.

Example:
Prompt: "A perfume bottle surrounded by swirling, colorful smoke, with abstract floral shapes emerging from the mist."

The image will highlight the product in a striking and artistic way, appealing to consumers' sense of wonder and imagination.

Practical Tips for Designing Fantastical and Surreal Scenes

Embrace Imagination:
Let your imagination run wild when crafting prompts for fantastical and surreal scenes. The more creative and unconventional, the better.

Example:
Prompt: "A giant jellyfish floating above a cityscape, its tentacles made of light and clouds swirling around it."

Mix Real and Unreal Elements:
Combining realistic and fantastical elements can create a compelling contrast that enhances the surreal quality of the image.

Example:
Prompt: "A realistic apple tree growing in the middle of a glowing, neon-colored desert under a starry sky."

Use Rich Descriptions:
Incorporate detailed and vivid descriptions to guide the AI in creating intricate and imaginative scenes.

Example:
Prompt: "A castle made of ice, with spires that reach the clouds and a moat filled with shimmering, liquid silver."

Experiment with Juxtapositions:
Juxtaposing unrelated elements can produce striking and thought-provoking surreal images.

Example:
Prompt: "A vintage typewriter with keys made of blooming flowers, sitting on a floating cloud in a pastel sky."

Iterate and Refine:
Experiment with different prompts and refine them to achieve the desired level of fantastical and surreal detail.

Example:
Initial Prompt: "A futuristic city." Refined Prompt: "A futuristic city with skyscrapers made of glass and light, hovering platforms, and rivers of molten metal flowing through the streets."

Designing fantastical and surreal scenes with DALL·E 3.0 allows for limitless creative exploration. By embracing imagination, mixing real and unreal elements, using rich descriptions, experimenting with juxtapositions, and iterating on your prompts, you can generate visually stunning and conceptually rich images. These techniques are invaluable for artists, writers, game designers, advertisers, and anyone looking to create unique and captivating visuals that transcend the ordinary.

Generating Character Designs

DALL·E 3.0 excels in generating detailed and imaginative character designs, making it an invaluable tool for artists, game developers, writers, and anyone involved in storytelling or creative projects. Whether you need realistic human characters, fantastical creatures, or stylized personas, DALL·E 3.0 can bring your ideas to life.

Game Development

Hero Characters:
Game developers can use DALL·E 3.0 to design hero characters with distinctive looks and personalities that stand out in gameplay.

Example:
Prompt: "A heroic warrior with silver armor, a blue cape, and a glowing sword, standing tall with a determined expression."

The generated image will depict a strong, visually striking character suitable for a fantasy or adventure game.

Villains and Antagonists:
Creating compelling villain characters with unique and intimidating appearances.

Example:
Prompt: "A dark sorcerer with glowing red eyes, a flowing black robe, and swirling dark energy around his hands."

The image will capture the menacing presence of a powerful antagonist, adding depth to the game's storyline.

Storytelling and Writing

Protagonists:
Writers can visualize their main characters to help develop their stories and make them more vivid and engaging.

Example:
Prompt: "A young detective with a keen eye, wearing a trench coat and fedora, with a magnifying glass in hand and a thoughtful expression."

The image will provide a detailed depiction of the protagonist, enhancing the narrative development process.

Supporting Characters:
Designing secondary characters that enrich the story and add complexity to the plot.

Example:
Prompt: "A wise old librarian with round glasses, a long gray beard, and a gentle smile, surrounded by ancient books in a cozy library."

The generated character can add depth and variety to the story's cast.

Comics and Graphic Novels

Main Heroes:
Graphic novelists can create distinctive main characters that appeal to readers and bring their stories to life.

Example:
Prompt: "A teenage superhero with a red and yellow costume, a confident stance, and energy beams emanating from his hands."

The image will depict a dynamic and visually engaging superhero character for a graphic novel.

Unique Sidekicks:
Designing unique sidekicks that complement the main characters and add intrigue to the storyline.

Example:
Prompt: "A quirky robot sidekick with a round body, antennae, and expressive LED eyes, floating beside the hero."

The image will create a memorable and appealing sidekick character.

Animation and Film

Animated Characters:
Animators can visualize characters that will be brought to life through animation, ensuring they have distinctive and expressive designs.

Example:
Prompt: "A cheerful animated cat with big green eyes, a striped tail, and a playful pose, ready for adventure."

The image will provide a clear design for an animated character, aiding in the animation process.

Fantasy Creatures:
Creating fantastical creatures for animated films or series, adding magic and wonder to the visuals.

Example:
Prompt: "A majestic dragon with shimmering blue scales, large wings, and a regal expression, perched on a cliff."

The image will help visualize a key fantasy creature for an animation project.

Fashion and Costume Design

Fashion Models:
Fashion designers can visualize new clothing designs on models to better understand how they will look in real life.

Example:
Prompt: "A tall fashion model wearing a sleek black evening gown with intricate gold embroidery, standing on a runway."

The image will provide a realistic depiction of the clothing design on a model.

Costume Concepts:
Designing costumes for film, theater, or cosplay with detailed and imaginative elements.

Example:
Prompt: "A medieval knight's armor with intricate engravings, a flowing cape, and a plumed helmet, ready for battle."

The image will offer a detailed costume design that can be used for production purposes.

Practical Tips for Generating Character Designs

Be Descriptive:
Include specific details about the character's appearance, attire, and accessories to guide the AI effectively.

Example:
Basic Prompt: "A pirate." *Detailed Prompt:* "A rugged pirate with a tricorn hat, a weathered face with a scar, a striped shirt, a leather belt with a sword, and a parrot on his shoulder."

Incorporate Personality Traits:
Describe the character's personality or role to add depth and context to the design.

Example:
Without Personality: "A teacher." *With Personality:* "A kind-hearted teacher with glasses, curly hair, a warm smile, and a stack of books in her arms."

Specify Artistic Styles:
If you have a particular artistic style in mind, include it in your prompt to achieve the desired visual effect.

Example:
Without Style: "A robot." *With Style:* "A retro-futuristic robot with a shiny chrome body, vintage dials, and blinking lights, in the style of 1950s sci-fi."

Combine Multiple Elements:
Combining different characteristics or themes can create unique and intriguing character designs.

Example:
"A futuristic samurai with cybernetic armor, a glowing katana, and a helmet with neon accents, standing in a neon-lit city."

Iterate and Refine:
Experiment with different prompts and refine them based on the generated results to achieve the perfect character design.

Example:
Initial Prompt: "A space explorer." Refined Prompt: "A space explorer with a sleek silver spacesuit, a helmet with a reflective visor, a jetpack, and a laser gun, standing on an alien planet."

Generating character designs with DALL·E 3.0 offers endless possibilities for creating detailed, imaginative, and distinctive characters for various applications. By being descriptive, incorporating personality traits, specifying artistic styles, combining multiple elements, and iterating on prompts, you can bring your character concepts to life in vivid and compelling ways. These techniques are invaluable for game developers, writers, animators, fashion designers, and anyone involved in creative projects that require unique and visually engaging characters.

Developing Landscapes and Environments

DALL·E 3.0 is an exceptional tool for creating detailed and immersive landscapes and environments, making it invaluable for artists, game developers, filmmakers, architects, and educators. Whether you need realistic settings or fantastical worlds, DALL·E 3.0 can bring your visions to life.

Game Development

Open-World Environments:
Game developers can create expansive and detailed open-world environments that enhance the gaming experience.

Example:
Prompt: "A vast desert landscape with rolling dunes, a distant oasis with palm trees, and ancient ruins partially buried in the sand under a blazing sun."

The generated image will depict a rich, immersive environment that players can explore, adding depth to the game's world.

Level Design:
Designing specific levels or areas within a game with unique and engaging settings.

Example:
Prompt: "A dark, enchanted forest with towering trees, glowing mushrooms, and a winding path leading to a hidden cave entrance."

The image will provide a visually captivating setting for a game level, enhancing the player's sense of adventure.

Film and Animation

Cinematic Landscapes:
Filmmakers can visualize stunning landscapes for use in movies, adding visual appeal and setting the tone for scenes.

Example:
Prompt: "A serene mountain valley at sunrise, with mist rising from a crystal-clear lake, surrounded by lush forests and towering peaks."

The image will capture the beauty and tranquility of the setting, perfect for establishing shots or key scenes in a film.

Animated Backgrounds:
Creating detailed backgrounds for animated films or series that add depth and context to the story.

Example:
Prompt: "A bustling futuristic city with skyscrapers, flying cars, neon signs, and elevated walkways connecting the buildings."

The generated image will provide a dynamic and detailed backdrop for an animated project.

Architectural Visualization

Urban Planning:
Urban planners can use DALL·E 3.0 to visualize new cityscapes and urban developments, aiding in the design and presentation process.

Example:
Prompt: "A modern urban park with green spaces, walking paths,

playgrounds, and a central fountain, surrounded by high-rise buildings and bustling streets."

The image will depict a well-designed urban space that integrates nature with city life.

Residential Design:
Architects can visualize residential environments, helping clients see how their future homes will look in different settings.

Example:
Prompt: "A cozy suburban neighborhood with tree-lined streets, single-family homes with front yards, and children playing outside under a clear blue sky."

The image will provide a realistic and appealing view of a potential residential development.

Art and Creative Projects

Fantasy Landscapes:
Artists can create fantastical landscapes for use in digital art, concept art, or illustrations.

Example:
Prompt: "A magical kingdom floating in the clouds, with golden castles, rainbow bridges, and mythical creatures flying in the sky."

The generated image will depict an enchanting and otherworldly scene, perfect for creative art projects.

Surreal Environments:
Designing surreal environments that challenge reality and provoke thought.

Example:
Prompt: "A dreamlike landscape with melting clocks hanging from

twisted trees, floating islands, and a sky filled with swirling colors."

The image will provide a visually striking and surreal setting, ideal for conceptual art.

Educational and Scientific Visualization

Geographical Illustrations:
Educators can use DALL·E 3.0 to create detailed illustrations of geographical features, aiding in teaching and learning.

Example:
Prompt: "A detailed cross-section of a volcanic island, showing the magma chamber, vents, and layers of rock, with an eruption in progress."

The image will help students understand geological processes through a clear and engaging visual.

Environmental Studies:
Visualizing different ecosystems and environmental scenarios to enhance understanding and awareness.

Example:
Prompt: "A tropical rainforest with dense vegetation, towering trees, diverse wildlife, and a river flowing through it."

The generated image will provide a comprehensive view of the ecosystem, useful for educational purposes.

Practical Tips for Developing Landscapes and Environments

Be Specific and Detailed:
Include as many details as possible about the environment's elements, such as terrain, vegetation, structures, and lighting.

Example:
Basic Prompt: "A beach." *Detailed Prompt:* "A pristine beach with

white sand, turquoise waters, gentle waves, palm trees, and a vibrant sunset casting warm hues over the scene."

Use Descriptive Language:
Employ rich descriptive language to enhance the visual richness of the environment.

Example:
Basic Prompt: "A forest." *Descriptive Prompt:* "A dense, ancient forest with towering oak trees, a carpet of moss and ferns, dappled sunlight filtering through the canopy, and a winding path leading deeper into the woods."

Incorporate Context and Theme:
Provide context or a theme to guide the AI in creating a coherent and meaningful environment.

Example:
Basic Prompt: "A city street." *Contextual Prompt:* "A busy Victorian-era city street with cobblestone roads, horse-drawn carriages, gas lamps, and people in period clothing."

Combine Real and Imaginary Elements:
Mix realistic and fantastical elements to create unique and imaginative environments.

Example:
"A desert landscape with giant crystal formations, ancient ruins, and a sky filled with two moons and swirling stars."

Iterate and Refine:
Experiment with different prompts and refine them based on the generated results to achieve the desired level of detail and coherence.

Example:
Initial Prompt: "A winter landscape." Refined Prompt: "A snowy

winter landscape with a frozen lake, snow-covered pine trees, a wooden cabin with smoke rising from the chimney, and a clear night sky filled with stars."

Developing landscapes and environments with DALL·E 3.0 involves using specific, descriptive, and contextual prompts to guide the AI effectively. By leveraging its capabilities, you can generate high-quality visuals for game development, film and animation, architectural visualization, art, and education. Mastering the art of crafting detailed and imaginative prompts will enable you to produce stunning and immersive landscapes and environments that meet your specific needs and enhance your projects.

Conclusion

DALL·E 3.0's versatility makes it an invaluable tool for a wide range of applications, from creating realistic and fantastical images to designing characters, landscapes, and educational illustrations. By understanding and leveraging its capabilities, users can produce high-quality visuals that meet their specific needs and enhance their projects. Whether for artistic, commercial, educational, or scientific purposes, DALL·E 3.0 offers endless possibilities for creative expression and visualization.

Chapter 6: Prompt Optimization

Optimizing your prompts is crucial for achieving high-quality, accurate, and visually compelling results with DALL·E 3.0. Well-optimized prompts help the AI understand your vision more clearly, resulting in images that closely match your expectations.

Importance of Prompt Optimization

Improving Image Quality:

Optimized prompts result in better image quality by providing the AI with clear, specific, and detailed instructions.

Example:

Non-optimized Prompt: "A city at night." *Optimized Prompt:* "A vibrant city skyline at night, with glowing skyscrapers, busy streets filled with car lights, and a clear, starry sky."

The optimized prompt includes more details, resulting in a richer and more detailed image.

Ensuring Accuracy:

Clear and detailed prompts help ensure that the generated images accurately reflect your vision, reducing the need for multiple iterations.

Example:

Non-optimized Prompt: "A mountain." *Optimized Prompt:* "A majestic snow-capped mountain peak, surrounded by a dense pine forest, with a crystal-clear lake at its base reflecting the mountain."

The optimized prompt provides a more accurate depiction of the desired scene.

Techniques for Prompt Optimization

Be Specific and Detailed:

Include specific details about the elements you want in the image. The more precise your description, the better the AI can understand and generate the desired result.

Example:

Non-optimized Prompt: "A garden." *Optimized Prompt:* "A lush garden filled with blooming roses, tulips, and daisies, with a cobblestone path winding through it and a white wooden bench under a large oak tree."

Use Descriptive Adjectives:

Employ descriptive adjectives to add depth and richness to your prompts. This helps convey the visual characteristics and atmosphere more effectively.

Example:

Non-optimized Prompt: "A car." *Optimized Prompt:* "A sleek, red sports car with shiny chrome details, parked on a winding mountain road, with the sun setting behind the peaks."

Provide Context and Background:

Contextual information helps the AI understand the relationships between different elements and how they fit together in the scene.

Example:

Non-optimized Prompt: "A person reading." *Optimized Prompt:* "A young woman with glasses, sitting in a cozy armchair by the fireplace, reading a hardcover book, with a cup of tea on a nearby table."

Incorporate Actions and Interactions:

Describing actions and interactions between elements adds dynamism and life to the image.

Example:

Non-optimized Prompt: "A dog in a park." *Optimized Prompt:* "A playful golden retriever running through a park, chasing a frisbee, with children playing in the background and cherry blossom trees in full bloom."

Specify Artistic Styles and Mediums:
Indicate if you want the image in a particular artistic style or medium to achieve the desired aesthetic effect.

Example:
Non-optimized Prompt: "A landscape." *Optimized Prompt:* "A serene landscape painted in the style of Impressionism, with soft, blurred brushstrokes, vibrant colors, and a focus on the play of light and shadow."

Experiment with Different Phrasings:
Try different ways of phrasing your prompt to see which yields the best results. Sometimes slight changes in wording can significantly impact the outcome.

Example:
Initial Prompt: "A futuristic city." Refined Prompt: "A bustling futuristic city with towering skyscrapers, flying cars, neon lights, and people in high-tech attire walking on elevated walkways."

Examples of Optimized Prompts

Example 1: From Basic to Detailed *Non-optimized Prompt:* "A forest." *Optimized Prompt:* "A dense forest with tall pine trees, a carpet of fallen leaves, a winding path, and sunlight filtering through the branches, creating dappled light on the ground."

Example 2: Adding Context and Actions *Non-optimized Prompt:* "A beach scene." *Optimized Prompt:* "A tropical beach with white sand, turquoise waters, palm trees, and a couple walking hand in hand along the shore, with a beach umbrella and towels nearby."

Example 3: Specifying Artistic Style *Non-optimized Prompt:* "A portrait of a woman." *Optimized Prompt:* "A portrait of a woman in the style of Renaissance oil painting, with detailed brushwork, realistic proportions, and a warm, glowing light."

Practical Tips for Prompt Optimization

Iterate and Refine:
Continuously refine your prompts based on the results you get. Start with a basic description and add details iteratively to improve the image quality.

Example:
Initial Prompt: "A mountain lake." Refined Prompt: "A clear mountain lake surrounded by pine trees, with a snow-capped mountain reflecting in the water, and a wooden dock extending into the lake."

Use Comparisons and Analogies:
Comparing elements to familiar objects or scenes can help the AI understand your vision better.

Example:
"A castle with towers that look like they are made of spun sugar, in a landscape that resembles a scene from a fairy tale."

Ask for Feedback:
If possible, seek feedback from others to identify areas where your prompts can be improved for clarity and detail.

Balance Detail with Simplicity:
While detail is important, avoid making prompts overly complex. Focus on the most critical elements to convey your vision clearly.

Example:
Overly Complex Prompt: "A bustling city with skyscrapers, parks, rivers, bridges, people, cars, animals, and various buildings."

Balanced Prompt: "A bustling city with towering skyscrapers, green parks, a river with arched bridges, and people walking along busy streets."

Iterative Refinement

Iterative refinement is a critical process in prompt optimization for DALL·E 3.0. This technique involves starting with a basic prompt and progressively adding details and modifications based on the results obtained. Iterative refinement helps achieve more precise, detailed, and high-quality images by allowing you to fine-tune your prompts step by step.

Importance of Iterative Refinement

Enhancing Detail and Accuracy:

Iterative refinement allows you to gradually add details to your prompts, improving the accuracy and quality of the generated images. This step-by-step approach helps ensure that the AI captures all the necessary elements and nuances.

Example:

Initial Prompt: "A mountain." *Refined Prompt:* "A snow-capped mountain peak with rugged cliffs, surrounded by a dense pine forest and a crystal-clear lake at its base."

Adapting to Results:

By reviewing the images generated from initial prompts, you can identify areas that need more detail or adjustments and refine your prompts accordingly. This adaptive process helps achieve the desired outcome more efficiently.

Example:

Initial Prompt: "A cat in a garden." *Refined Prompt:* "A fluffy white cat sitting on a stone path in a colorful garden filled with blooming flowers and butterflies."

Techniques for Iterative Refinement

Start with a Basic Prompt:
Begin with a simple and straightforward description of the scene or subject you want to generate. This provides a foundation upon which you can build more details.

Example:
Basic Prompt: "A beach at sunset."

Add Incremental Details:
Gradually add specific details and elements to your prompt, enhancing the complexity and richness of the image.

Example:
First Refinement: "A tropical beach at sunset with white sand and palm trees." *Second Refinement:* "A tropical beach at sunset with white sand, palm trees, gentle waves, and a beach umbrella with a couple sitting underneath."

Incorporate Feedback from Results:
Review the images generated by each version of your prompt and note any aspects that need improvement or additional detail. Use this feedback to refine your prompt further.

Example:
Initial Result: The image shows a beach but lacks depth. *Refined Prompt:* "A tropical beach at sunset with white sand, palm trees, gentle waves, a beach umbrella with a couple sitting underneath, and a sailboat on the horizon."

Experiment with Different Phrasings:
Try different ways of phrasing your prompt to see which produces the best results. This helps identify the most effective language for conveying your vision.

Example:
Initial Prompt: "A futuristic city." *Refined Prompt:* "A bustling futuristic city with neon-lit skyscrapers, flying cars, and people walking on elevated walkways."

Examples of Iterative Refinement

Example 1: Developing a Landscape *Basic Prompt:* "A forest." *First Refinement:* "A dense forest with tall pine trees." *Second Refinement:* "A dense forest with tall pine trees and a carpet of fallen leaves." *Third Refinement:* "A dense forest with tall pine trees, a carpet of fallen leaves, a winding path, and sunlight filtering through the branches."

Example 2: Creating a Character *Basic Prompt:* "A wizard." *First Refinement:* "A wizard with a long beard and a robe." *Second Refinement:* "A wizard with a long white beard, a blue robe with silver stars, and a pointed hat." *Third Refinement:* "A wizard with a long white beard, a blue robe with silver stars, a pointed hat, and holding a glowing staff."

Example 3: Designing an Environment *Basic Prompt:* "A city street." *First Refinement:* "A busy city street with tall buildings." *Second Refinement:* "A busy city street with tall buildings and people walking on the sidewalks." *Third Refinement:* "A busy city street with tall buildings, people walking on the sidewalks, street vendors selling food, and cars driving by."

Practical Tips for Iterative Refinement

Review and Analyze Results:
Carefully review the images generated from each iteration to identify what works well and what needs improvement. Look for elements that may be missing or incorrectly rendered and refine your prompt accordingly.

Example:
If the initial image lacks the desired level of detail in the background, add more specific elements in your next iteration to enhance depth and context.

Be Patient and Methodical:
Iterative refinement is a process that requires patience and attention to detail. Take your time to gradually build up the complexity of your prompt, ensuring each addition contributes meaningfully to the final image.

Example:
Instead of adding all desired details at once, introduce elements one by one and assess their impact on the overall image quality.

Use Clear and Descriptive Language:
As you refine your prompt, use clear and descriptive language to convey specific visual elements. This helps the AI understand and accurately render your vision.

Example:
Instead of simply describing "a house," specify "a quaint cottage with a thatched roof, ivy climbing the walls, and a flower garden in the front yard."

Combine Multiple Refinements:
In some cases, combining several refinements into a single prompt can lead to more cohesive and detailed images.

Example:
Final Prompt: "A cozy cottage with a thatched roof, ivy climbing the walls, a flower garden in the front yard, and a wooden fence surrounding the property, under a clear blue sky with birds flying."

Iterative refinement is a powerful technique for optimizing prompts and achieving high-quality, accurate images with DALL·E 3.0. By starting with a basic prompt, adding incremental details, incorporating feedback from results, and experimenting with different phrasings, you can progressively refine your prompts to better convey your vision. Patience, careful analysis, and clear descriptive language are key to successfully using iterative refinement to create stunning and detailed images that meet your specific needs and expectations.

Analyzing Generated Outputs

Analyzing the outputs generated by DALL·E 3.0 is a crucial step in optimizing your prompts. This process involves evaluating the quality, accuracy, and relevance of the images produced in response to your prompts and using this information to refine and improve subsequent prompts. By systematically analyzing generated outputs, you can identify areas for improvement and achieve better results.

Importance of Analyzing Generated Outputs

Ensuring Quality and Accuracy:
By analyzing the generated images, you can assess how well the outputs match your vision and identify any discrepancies. This helps ensure that the final images are of high quality and accurately represent the intended scene or subject.

Example:
Prompt: "A serene beach at sunset with palm trees and a hammock."
Analysis: The generated image includes a beach and sunset but lacks palm trees and a hammock. The prompt needs refinement to emphasize these missing elements.

Identifying Areas for Improvement:
Evaluating the outputs allows you to pinpoint specific areas that

need more detail, better clarity, or adjustments to match your expectations.

Example:
Prompt: "A bustling city street at night with neon lights."
Analysis: The image captures the city street and neon lights but appears too dark and lacks detail in the buildings. Refinement should focus on enhancing the visibility and detail of the buildings.

Techniques for Analyzing Generated Outputs

Compare Outputs to Prompts:
Compare the generated images to the original prompts to see how well they align. Check if all specified elements are present and accurately depicted.

Example:
Prompt: "A snowy mountain landscape with a log cabin and a smoke-filled chimney."
Analysis: Ensure the image includes the snowy mountains, log cabin, and smoke from the chimney as described.

Assess Detail and Clarity:
Evaluate the level of detail and clarity in the images. Look for any areas that appear blurry, incomplete, or lacking in detail.

Example:
Prompt: "A detailed cross-section of a volcano showing magma chambers and lava flow."
Analysis: Verify that the cross-section is clear, with well-defined magma chambers and visible lava flow paths.

Check for Consistency and Coherence:
Ensure that the elents in the image are consistent with each other and create a coherent scene. Look for any mismatched or out-of-place elements.

Example:
Prompt: "A medieval marketplace with vendors, stalls, and townsfolk."
Analysis: Confirm that all elements fit the medieval theme and that the scene appears coherent, with vendors and stalls matching the historical context.

Evaluate Artistic and Aesthetic Quality:
Assess the artistic and aesthetic quality of the images. Consider factors such as composition, color balance, and overall visual appeal.

Example:
Prompt: "A vibrant garden with colorful flowers and butterflies."
Analysis: Check that the image is visually appealing, with a balanced composition and a harmonious mix of colors.

Examples of Analyzing Generated Outputs

Example 1: Landscape Analysis *Prompt:* "A lush forest with a river flowing through it and a deer drinking water." *Generated Output:* The image includes a forest and river but no deer.
Analysis: The prompt needs refinement to emphasize the inclusion of the deer.
Refined Prompt: "A lush forest with tall trees, a river flowing through it, and a deer drinking water by the riverbank."

Example 2: Character Design Analysis *Prompt:* "A knight in shining armor standing in front of a castle." *Generated Output:* The image includes a knight and castle, but the armor lacks detail.
Analysis: The prompt should specify the desired details for the armor to enhance its visual quality.
Refined Prompt: "A knight in detailed, shining armor with intricate engravings, standing in front of a grand medieval castle."

Example 3: Environmental Design Analysis *Prompt:* "A futuristic city with flying cars and neon signs." *Generated Output:* The image captures the futuristic city and neon signs but lacks flying cars. *Analysis:* The prompt needs more emphasis on the flying cars to ensure their inclusion.
Refined Prompt: "A bustling futuristic city with tall skyscrapers, neon signs, and numerous flying cars zipping through the air."

Practical Tips for Analyzing Generated Outputs

Take Notes:
Keep detailed notes on the aspects of the generated images that meet your expectations and those that do not. This documentation will help guide your refinements.

Example:
Note that the cityscape has the right lighting and atmosphere but needs more detailed building designs.

Use a Checklist:
Create a checklist of the key elements and criteria specified in your prompt. Use this checklist to systematically evaluate the generated images.

Example:
For a prompt about a forest scene, the checklist might include: dense trees, a clear river, wildlife, and sunlight filtering through the canopy.

Seek Feedback:
If possible, seek feedback from others to get different perspectives on the quality and accuracy of the generated images. This can provide additional insights for refinement.

Example:
Show the generated images to a colleague and ask for their input on the detail and coherence of the scene.

Iterate Based on Analysis:
Use the findings from your analysis to iteratively refine your prompts. Make specific adjustments to address any issues identified during the evaluation.

Example:
If the analysis reveals that the image lacks detail in the background, refine the prompt to specify additional background elements such as distant mountains or a sunset sky.

Analyzing generated outputs is a critical step in optimizing prompts for DALL·E 3.0. By comparing outputs to prompts, assessing detail and clarity, checking for consistency and coherence, and evaluating artistic and aesthetic quality, you can identify areas for improvement and refine your prompts accordingly. Taking notes, using checklists, seeking feedback, and iterating based on analysis will help you achieve high-quality, accurate, and visually compelling images that meet your expectations and project requirements.

Adjusting Prompts Based on Feedback

Adjusting prompts based on feedback is an essential aspect of prompt optimization for DALL·E 3.0. Feedback provides valuable insights into the strengths and weaknesses of generated images, helping you refine your prompts to achieve better results. This process involves collecting feedback, analyzing it, and making specific adjustments to your prompts to improve the quality and accuracy of the outputs.

Importance of Adjusting Prompts Based on Feedback

Improving Precision and Detail:
Feedback helps identify areas where the generated images lack

precision or detail. Adjusting prompts based on this feedback ensures that all desired elements are accurately represented.

Example:
Initial Prompt: "A cat on a windowsill." *Feedback:* The cat is not detailed enough, and the windowsill lacks context. *Adjusted Prompt:* "A fluffy white cat with blue eyes, sitting on a sunlit wooden windowsill with a view of a blooming garden."

Enhancing Relevance and Coherence:
Feedback can highlight inconsistencies or irrelevant elements in the images. Adjusting prompts based on this feedback helps create more coherent and contextually relevant images.

Example:
Initial Prompt: "A medieval knight." *Feedback:* The armor looks too modern, and the background is not appropriate. *Adjusted Prompt:* "A medieval knight in detailed, traditional armor, standing in front of a stone castle with banners and a moat."

Techniques for Adjusting Prompts Based on Feedback

Collect Detailed Feedback:
Gather detailed feedback from multiple sources, including peers, clients, or end-users. Focus on specific aspects such as accuracy, detail, composition, and overall impression.

Example:
Feedback might include comments like, "The background looks too plain," or "The colors are not vibrant enough."

Identify Common Themes:
Look for common themes or recurring issues in the feedback. These patterns will help you prioritize the most critical adjustments needed.

Example:
If multiple people mention that the image lacks depth, focus on adding more background and foreground elements.

Make Specific Adjustments:
Based on the feedback, make specific and targeted adjustments to your prompts. Be clear and detailed about the changes you want to see.

Example:
Feedback: "The scene looks too dark." *Adjusted Prompt:* "A bright, sunlit forest with tall trees, a clear river, and dappled sunlight filtering through the leaves."

Test Adjusted Prompts:
After making adjustments, test the new prompts by generating images and comparing them to the feedback. Repeat the process as needed until the images meet the desired standards.

Example:
Generate a new image based on the adjusted prompt and review it to ensure it addresses the feedback about brightness and detail.

Examples of Adjusting Prompts Based on Feedback

Example 1: Landscape Adjustment *Initial Prompt:* "A mountain lake." *Feedback:* The lake looks too small, and the mountains lack detail. *Adjusted Prompt:* "A large, crystal-clear mountain lake surrounded by detailed, snow-capped peaks and a dense pine forest."

Example 2: Character Design Adjustment *Initial Prompt:* "A wizard casting a spell." *Feedback:* The spell effect is not visible, and the wizard's robes lack detail. *Adjusted Prompt:* "A wise wizard with a long white beard, wearing detailed blue robes with silver runes, casting a glowing spell with swirling magical energy."

Example 3: Environmental Design Adjustment *Initial Prompt:* "A futuristic city street." *Feedback:* The street looks too empty, and the buildings are not futuristic enough. *Adjusted Prompt:* "A bustling futuristic city street with neon-lit skyscrapers, flying cars, and people walking on elevated walkways."

Practical Tips for Adjusting Prompts Based on Feedback

Be Open to Criticism:
Approach feedback with an open mind and a willingness to make changes. Constructive criticism is a valuable tool for improving your prompts and achieving better results.

Example:
Consider all feedback carefully, even if it means making significant changes to your initial vision.

Prioritize Adjustments:
Not all feedback will be equally important. Prioritize adjustments that address the most critical issues or that are mentioned by multiple sources.

Example:
If several reviewers mention that the colors are dull, prioritize enhancing the color vibrancy in your prompt adjustments.

Keep Iterating:
Prompt optimization is an iterative process. Continue refining your prompts based on new feedback until you achieve the desired results.

Example:
Generate multiple versions of the adjusted prompt, incorporating ongoing feedback to continuously improve the image quality.

Document Changes:
Keep track of the adjustments you make and the corresponding

feedback. This documentation will help you understand what works and why, aiding future prompt optimization efforts.

Example:
Create a log of each prompt version, the feedback received, and the specific changes made in response.

Adjusting prompts based on feedback is a critical step in optimizing your interactions with DALL·E 3.0. By collecting detailed feedback, identifying common themes, making specific adjustments, and testing the results, you can refine your prompts to achieve high-quality, accurate, and visually appealing images. Being open to criticism, prioritizing adjustments, iterating continuously, and documenting changes will help you effectively use feedback to improve your prompt optimization process.

Conclusion

Prompt optimization is essential for harnessing the full potential of DALL·E 3.0 and achieving high-quality, accurate images. By being specific and detailed, using descriptive adjectives, providing context and background, incorporating actions and interactions, specifying artistic styles, and experimenting with different phrasings, you can create optimized prompts that effectively communicate your vision to the AI. Iterative refinement and balancing detail with simplicity will further enhance the quality of the generated images, ensuring they meet your expectations and project requirements.

Chapter 7: Troubleshooting and Problem Solving

Creating high-quality images with DALL·E 3.0 involves not only crafting detailed prompts but also addressing any issues that arise during the generation process. Troubleshooting and problem solving are essential skills to ensure that the outputs meet your expectations.

Common Issues and Solutions

1. Incomplete or Missing Elements

Issue:
The generated image lacks key elements specified in the prompt.

Solution:
Revisit your prompt to ensure it includes clear and specific descriptions of all desired elements. Emphasize any missing components in the refined prompt.

Example:
Initial Prompt: "A beach with a lighthouse." *Generated Output:* The beach is present, but the lighthouse is missing. *Refined Prompt:* "A beach with white sand and gentle waves, featuring a tall, white lighthouse with a red roof standing on a rocky outcrop."

2. Lack of Detail

Issue:
The generated image appears too simplistic or lacks sufficient detail.

Solution:
Enhance your prompt with more descriptive language and additional details to provide a clearer vision for the AI.

Example:

Initial Prompt: "A forest." *Generated Output:* The forest looks too plain. *Refined Prompt:* "A dense forest with towering pine trees, a carpet of vibrant green moss, scattered wildflowers, and sunlight filtering through the canopy."

3. Inconsistent Style or Theme

Issue:

The elements in the generated image do not match the desired style or theme, resulting in an incoherent scene.

Solution:

Specify the style or theme more clearly in your prompt and ensure all elements align with it.

Example:

Initial Prompt: "A medieval village." *Generated Output:* The village includes modern elements, like cars. *Refined Prompt:* "A medieval village with cobblestone streets, thatched-roof cottages, villagers in period clothing, and horse-drawn carts."

4. Unnatural or Uncanny Results

Issue:

The generated image features elements that look unnatural or uncanny, particularly in human faces or anatomical features.

Solution:

Refine your prompt to emphasize natural and realistic features, and consider simplifying the description to focus on key elements.

Example:

Initial Prompt: "A smiling child." *Generated Output:* The child's face looks distorted. *Refined Prompt:* "A young child with curly brown hair, bright blue eyes, and a natural, joyful smile."

5. Overcrowded or Cluttered Composition

Issue:
The generated image appears too busy or cluttered, with too many elements competing for attention.

Solution:
Simplify your prompt by focusing on the most important elements and reducing unnecessary details.

Example:
Initial Prompt: "A busy market scene with stalls, people, food, decorations, and animals." *Generated Output:* The scene looks overcrowded and chaotic. *Refined Prompt:* "A lively market scene with colorful stalls selling fruits and vegetables, a few shoppers browsing, and a street musician playing a guitar."

6. Incorrect Colors or Lighting

Issue:
The colors or lighting in the generated image do not match the desired mood or setting.

Solution:
Specify the desired colors and lighting conditions more explicitly in your prompt.

Example:
Initial Prompt: "A sunset over the ocean." *Generated Output:* The colors are dull and the lighting is incorrect. *Refined Prompt:* "A vibrant sunset over the ocean, with the sky ablaze in shades of orange, pink, and purple, and the water reflecting the warm, golden light."

7. Misinterpreted Actions or Interactions

Issue:
The generated image does not correctly depict actions or interactions between elements.

Solution:
Clarify and detail the actions or interactions in your prompt to ensure accurate representation.

Example:
Initial Prompt: "A dog playing with a ball." *Generated Output:* The dog and ball are present, but they are not interacting. *Refined Prompt:* "A playful golden retriever chasing and catching a red ball in mid-air in a grassy park."

Practical Tips for Troubleshooting and Problem Solving

Analyze Generated Outputs Critically:
Carefully examine the generated images to identify specific issues. Note any missing elements, inconsistencies, or areas lacking detail.

Example:
If the image of a "busy street" lacks people, note this as a key issue to address in the refined prompt.

Break Down Complex Scenes:
If the scene is too complex, break it down into simpler parts and refine each part individually before combining them.

Example:
Instead of describing an entire "festival," start with "a stage with musicians playing" and "crowds enjoying the music" separately.

Use Step-by-Step Refinements:
Make incremental adjustments to your prompt, testing each refinement to see how it improves the image quality.

Example:
Start with "a castle" and refine to "a grand medieval castle with tall towers, a drawbridge, and a surrounding moat."

Experiment with Different Descriptions:
Try different phrasings or synonyms to see if they yield better

results. Sometimes, a slight change in wording can make a significant difference.

Example:
Instead of "a person reading," try "a young woman engrossed in a book, sitting by a cozy fireplace."

Seek External Feedback:
Show the generated images to others to get additional perspectives on potential issues and areas for improvement.

Example:
If colleagues suggest that the "forest" scene looks too sparse, add more details like "thick underbrush and scattered wildflowers."

Document Your Process:
Keep a record of the prompts you use, the feedback received, and the adjustments made. This documentation will help you refine your approach over time.

Example:
Note each version of the prompt for "a city street," the changes made, and the resulting improvements in image quality.

Addressing Common Issues

When using DALL·E 3.0 to generate images, you may encounter a variety of common issues that can affect the quality and accuracy of the outputs. Effectively troubleshooting and solving these issues is key to achieving the best results.

Common Issues and Solutions

1. Incomplete or Missing Elements

Issue:
The generated image lacks key elements specified in the prompt.

Solution:
Revisit the prompt to ensure it includes clear and specific descriptions of all desired elements. Emphasize any missing components.

Example:
Initial Prompt: "A beach with a lighthouse." *Generated Output:* The beach is present, but the lighthouse is missing. *Refined Prompt:* "A beach with white sand and gentle waves, featuring a tall, white lighthouse with a red roof standing on a rocky outcrop."

2. Lack of Detail

Issue:
The generated image appears too simplistic or lacks sufficient detail.

Solution:
Enhance the prompt with more descriptive language and additional details to provide a clearer vision for the AI.

Example:
Initial Prompt: "A forest." *Generated Output:* The forest looks too plain. *Refined Prompt:* "A dense forest with towering pine trees, a carpet of vibrant green moss, scattered wildflowers, and sunlight filtering through the canopy."

3. Inconsistent Style or Theme

Issue:
The elements in the generated image do not match the desired style or theme, resulting in an incoherent scene.

Solution:
Specify the style or theme more clearly in the prompt and ensure all elements align with it.

Example:
Initial Prompt: "A medieval village." *Generated Output:* The village includes modern elements, like cars. *Refined Prompt:* "A medieval village with cobblestone streets, thatched-roof cottages, villagers in period clothing, and horse-drawn carts."

4. Unnatural or Uncanny Results

Issue:
The generated image features elements that look unnatural or uncanny, particularly in human faces or anatomical features.

Solution:
Refine the prompt to emphasize natural and realistic features, and consider simplifying the description to focus on key elements.

Example:
Initial Prompt: "A smiling child." *Generated Output:* The child's face looks distorted. *Refined Prompt:* "A young child with curly brown hair, bright blue eyes, and a natural, joyful smile."

5. Overcrowded or Cluttered Composition

Issue:
The generated image appears too busy or cluttered, with too many elements competing for attention.

Solution:
Simplify the prompt by focusing on the most important elements and reducing unnecessary details.

Example:
Initial Prompt: "A busy market scene with stalls, people, food, decorations, and animals." *Generated Output:* The scene looks overcrowded and chaotic. *Refined Prompt:* "A lively market scene with colorful stalls selling fruits and vegetables, a few shoppers browsing, and a street musician playing a guitar."

6. Incorrect Colors or Lighting

Issue:
The colors or lighting in the generated image do not match the desired mood or setting.

Solution:
Specify the desired colors and lighting conditions more explicitly in the prompt.

Example:
Initial Prompt: "A sunset over the ocean." *Generated Output:* The colors are dull and the lighting is incorrect. *Refined Prompt:* "A vibrant sunset over the ocean, with the sky ablaze in shades of orange, pink, and purple, and the water reflecting the warm, golden light."

7. Misinterpreted Actions or Interactions

Issue:
The generated image does not correctly depict actions or interactions between elements.

Solution:
Clarify and detail the actions or interactions in the prompt to ensure accurate representation.

Example:
Initial Prompt: "A dog playing with a ball." *Generated Output:* The dog and ball are present, but they are not interacting. *Refined Prompt:* "A playful golden retriever chasing and catching a red ball in mid-air in a grassy park."

Practical Tips for Troubleshooting and Problem Solving

Analyze Generated Outputs Critically:
Carefully examine the generated images to identify specific issues. Note any missing elements, inconsistencies, or areas lacking detail.

Example:
If the image of a "busy street" lacks people, note this as a key issue to address in the refined prompt.

Break Down Complex Scenes:
If the scene is too complex, break it down into simpler parts and refine each part individually before combining them.

Example:
Instead of describing an entire "festival," start with "a stage with musicians playing" and "crowds enjoying the music" separately.

Use Step-by-Step Refinements:
Make incremental adjustments to your prompt, testing each refinement to see how it improves the image quality.

Example:
Start with "a castle" and refine to "a grand medieval castle with tall towers, a drawbridge, and a surrounding moat."

Experiment with Different Descriptions:
Try different phrasings or synonyms to see if they yield better results. Sometimes, a slight change in wording can make a significant difference.

Example:
Instead of "a person reading," try "a young woman engrossed in a book, sitting by a cozy fireplace."

Seek External Feedback:
Show the generated images to others to get additional perspectives on potential issues and areas for improvement.

Example:
If colleagues suggest that the "forest" scene looks too sparse, add more details like "thick underbrush and scattered wildflowers."

Document Your Process:
Keep a record of the prompts you use, the feedback received, and the adjustments made. This documentation will help you understand what works and why, aiding future prompt optimization efforts.

Example:
Note each version of the prompt for "a city street," the changes made, and the resulting improvements in image quality.

Troubleshooting and problem solving are essential for optimizing prompts and achieving high-quality images with DALL·E 3.0. By critically analyzing generated outputs, making specific adjustments based on identified issues, and using iterative refinements, you can address common problems such as incomplete elements, lack of detail, inconsistent styles, unnatural results, overcrowded compositions, incorrect colors or lighting, and misinterpreted actions. Employing practical tips and seeking external feedback will further enhance your ability to refine prompts and create visually compelling, accurate, and detailed images that meet your needs and expectations.

Handling Unexpected Results

When working with DALL·E 3.0, it's common to encounter unexpected results that don't align with your vision. These results can range from minor deviations to completely off-target images. Handling these surprises effectively is key to optimizing your prompts and achieving the desired outcomes.

Understanding the Nature of Unexpected Results

Unexpected results occur when:

- The AI misinterprets the prompt.

- The generated image includes unintended elements.

- The style or composition deviates from expectations.

- Specific details are exaggerated or omitted.

Understanding why these issues arise helps in crafting better prompts and refining your approach.

Strategies for Handling Unexpected Results

1. Clarify and Simplify the Prompt

Issue:
The generated image includes elements that were not intended or misinterprets the prompt.

Solution:
Simplify and clarify your prompt. Remove ambiguous language and ensure the instructions are straightforward.

Example:
Initial Prompt: "A magical forest with a stream and fairies."
Generated Output: Includes elements like dragons and castles, which were not intended. *Refined Prompt:* "A serene forest with a clear stream, where small, glowing fairies fly around, under a canopy of tall trees."

2. Refine Descriptions

Issue:
The image includes elements that are close to but not exactly what was envisioned.

Solution:
Provide more detailed and precise descriptions of the desired elements.

Example:

Initial Prompt: "A modern kitchen." *Generated Output:* The kitchen looks generic and lacks specific features. *Refined Prompt:* "A modern kitchen with stainless steel appliances, a white marble island, pendant lighting, and wooden cabinets."

3. Use Specific Visual Cues

Issue:

The style or visual appearance does not match the desired aesthetic.

Solution:

Incorporate specific visual cues and references to guide the AI toward the correct style.

Example:

Initial Prompt: "A beach at sunrise." *Generated Output:* The colors and lighting are off. *Refined Prompt:* "A tranquil beach at sunrise, with soft pink and orange hues in the sky, gentle waves, and the sun just peeking over the horizon."

4. Break Down Complex Prompts

Issue:

The image is cluttered or the AI struggles with the complexity of the prompt.

Solution:

Break down the complex prompt into simpler parts and combine them in the final image.

Example:

Initial Prompt: "A busy city street with people, cars, buildings, and shops." *Generated Output:* The scene is too chaotic and lacks focus. *Refined Prompt:*

1. "A busy city street with tall buildings and shops."

2. "People walking on the sidewalks."

3. "Cars driving along the street."

5. Iterative Refinement

Issue:
The image requires multiple changes to meet the desired outcome.

Solution:
Use iterative refinement to gradually improve the prompt based on feedback from each generated image.

Example:
Initial Prompt: "A fantasy castle." *Generated Output:* The castle looks too futuristic. *Refined Prompt:* "A grand fantasy castle with stone walls, tall towers, and medieval architecture."

6. Incorporate Feedback Loops

Issue:
You consistently receive unexpected results even after refinements.

Solution:
Establish feedback loops by reviewing each image carefully, noting discrepancies, and adjusting the prompt accordingly.

Example:
Initial Prompt: "A pirate ship on the ocean." *Generated Output:* The ship lacks pirate-specific details. *Refined Prompt:* "A wooden pirate ship with tattered sails, a Jolly Roger flag, and cannons on the deck, sailing on a stormy ocean."

Practical Tips for Handling Unexpected Results

Be Patient and Persistent:
Unexpected results are part of the creative process. Patience and persistence are key to refining your prompts and achieving the desired outcomes.

Example:
If the first few iterations of a "mystical forest" don't capture the intended atmosphere, keep adjusting the prompt and re-evaluating the results.

Document Each Iteration:
Keep track of each prompt iteration and the corresponding results. This documentation helps identify what changes lead to better results.

Example:
Maintain a log of all attempts to create a "Victorian-era street," noting what each iteration improved or missed.

Use Comparative Analysis:
Compare the unexpected results with the desired outcome to understand where the discrepancies lie and adjust accordingly.

Example:
If a "sunset over a lake" is consistently too dark, compare it with reference images and adjust the prompt to emphasize lighter tones and reflections.

Seek Inspiration and References:
Use visual references and inspirations to guide the AI more accurately, ensuring it understands the desired outcome.

Example:
Include a reference to a specific art style or well-known image when trying to create a "surreal dreamscape."

Handling unexpected results is a crucial aspect of optimizing prompts for DALL·E 3.0. By clarifying and simplifying prompts, refining descriptions, using specific visual cues, breaking down complex prompts, applying iterative refinement, and incorporating feedback loops, you can systematically address and resolve common issues. Patience, persistence, and careful documentation of each step will help you navigate the challenges and achieve high-quality, accurate, and visually appealing images.

<u>Dealing With Limitations of DALL·E 3.0</u>

While DALL·E 3.0 is a powerful AI tool for generating images from textual descriptions, it has certain limitations that can impact the quality and accuracy of the outputs. Understanding these limitations and learning how to work around them is essential for optimizing your use of the AI.

Common Limitations and Solutions

1. Difficulty with Complex Scenes

Limitation:
DALL·E 3.0 may struggle to accurately render complex scenes with multiple interacting elements.

Solution:
Break down complex scenes into simpler, individual components and then combine them to form the complete scene.

Example:
Initial Prompt: "A crowded market with stalls, people shopping, children playing, and street performers." *Generated Output:* The scene is chaotic and lacks focus. *Refined Approach:*

1. "A market stall selling fruits and vegetables."

2. "People shopping at the market."

3. "Children playing near the market."

4. "A street performer entertaining the crowd."

By generating each component separately, you can ensure clarity and then manually combine them into a cohesive scene.

2. Handling Abstract Concepts

Limitation:
DALL·E 3.0 may have difficulty interpreting and visualizing abstract or conceptual ideas.

Solution:
Use concrete and descriptive language to represent abstract concepts, and provide clear visual cues or metaphors.

Example:
Initial Prompt: "The feeling of freedom." *Generated Output:* The image is vague and not representative. *Refined Prompt:* "A soaring eagle flying high above a vast, open landscape with a clear blue sky, symbolizing freedom."

By grounding the abstract concept in concrete imagery, you help the AI produce a more accurate representation.

3. Generating Human Faces

Limitation:
DALL·E 3.0 may produce human faces that look unnatural or distorted.

Solution:
Simplify the description of facial features and focus on the overall appearance and context rather than detailed facial specifics.

Example:
Initial Prompt: "A smiling woman with green eyes and a sharp nose." *Generated Output:* The face looks unnatural. *Refined Prompt:* "A cheerful woman with flowing brown hair, sitting in a sunlit garden, enjoying a sunny day."

By providing a broader context and less detailed facial features, you can achieve more natural-looking human faces.

4. Managing Lighting and Shadows

Limitation:
The AI may struggle to correctly interpret complex lighting and shadow scenarios.

Solution:
Provide explicit descriptions of the desired lighting conditions and the effects of shadows.

Example:
Initial Prompt: "A forest with sunlight." *Generated Output:* The lighting is inconsistent. *Refined Prompt:* "A dense forest with tall trees, where sunlight filters through the canopy, casting dappled shadows on the forest floor."

Describing the lighting effects in detail helps the AI render them more accurately.

5. Maintaining Stylistic Consistency

Limitation:
DALL·E 3.0 may have difficulty maintaining a consistent artistic style throughout an image.

Solution:
Specify the desired style clearly and consistently throughout the prompt, and provide examples if possible.

Example:
Initial Prompt: "A painting of a landscape." *Generated Output:* The style is inconsistent. *Refined Prompt:* "A landscape painting in the style of Impressionism, with soft, blurred brushstrokes and vibrant colors capturing the play of light and shadow."

By emphasizing the style, you guide the AI to produce a more consistent artistic output.

6. Handling Text within Images

Limitation:
DALL·E 3.0 often struggles to accurately generate readable text within images.

Solution:
Avoid relying on the AI to generate text within images. Instead, add text manually using graphic design tools after generating the image.

Example:
Initial Prompt: "A poster with the text 'Summer Festival.'"
Generated Output: The text is unreadable. *Refined Approach:* "A colorful poster for a summer festival, with space for text at the top."

Generate the image with a blank space for text and add the text later using an editing tool.

Practical Tips for Dealing with Limitations

Be Clear and Specific:
Clarity and specificity in your prompts help mitigate some of the AI's limitations by providing detailed guidance on what you want to achieve.

Example:
General Prompt: "A beach." *Specific Prompt:* "A sandy beach with turquoise waves gently lapping at the shore, under a clear blue sky with a few fluffy clouds."

Iterate and Refine:
Use iterative refinement to gradually improve the results, making small adjustments based on the generated outputs.

Example:
Start with "a beach scene" and refine to "a beach scene with a palm tree, sun loungers, and a beach ball."

Use Visual References:
When dealing with stylistic or complex visual elements, providing visual references can help the AI understand your vision better.

Example:
Describe a scene as "similar to the Art Nouveau style with flowing lines and organic shapes."

Combine Manual Editing:
For elements that the AI struggles with, such as text or precise details, use manual editing tools to refine the final image.

Example:
Generate the main image and then add text or fine details using graphic design software.

Understand and Accept Limitations:
Recognize the AI's limitations and adjust your expectations and prompts accordingly. Sometimes, simplifying your vision can lead to better results.

Example:
Instead of a highly detailed, multi-element scene, focus on a simpler, more impactful image.

Dealing with the limitations of DALL·E 3.0 involves understanding its strengths and weaknesses and employing strategies to work around its challenges. By clarifying and simplifying prompts, using concrete and descriptive language, iterating based on results, providing visual references, combining manual editing, and adjusting expectations, you can effectively handle common issues and optimize your use of the AI. These strategies will help you achieve high-quality, accurate, and visually compelling images that meet your needs and project requirements.

Conclusion

Troubleshooting and problem solving are essential for optimizing prompts and achieving high-quality images with DALL·E 3.0. By critically analyzing generated outputs, making specific adjustments based on identified issues, and using iterative refinements, you can address common problems such as incomplete elements, lack of detail, inconsistent styles, unnatural results, overcrowded compositions, incorrect colors or lighting, and misinterpreted actions. Employing practical tips and seeking external feedback will further enhance your ability to refine prompts and create visually compelling, accurate, and detailed images that meet your needs and expectations.

Chapter 8: Ethics and Responsible Use

The use of powerful AI tools like DALL·E 3.0 comes with significant ethical considerations. Ensuring that the technology is used responsibly is crucial to avoid potential misuse, harm, or unintended consequences.

Key Ethical Principles

1. Avoiding Harmful Content

Principle:
Do not use DALL·E 3.0 to create images that depict or promote violence, discrimination, hatred, or any form of harm.

Example:
Unethical Prompt: "An image showing a fight between two groups based on ethnicity." *Ethical Prompt:* "An image showing people from diverse backgrounds working together in harmony."

By focusing on positive and constructive themes, you ensure that the content generated is respectful and inclusive.

2. Respecting Privacy and Consent

Principle:
Avoid generating images of real individuals without their consent, especially in contexts that could harm their reputation or privacy.

Example:
Unethical Prompt: "A photo of a famous person in a compromising situation." *Ethical Prompt:* "A painting of a fictional character in a serene landscape."

Using fictional characters or anonymized subjects helps maintain privacy and respect for individuals.

3. Avoiding Misinformation

Principle:
Do not use DALL·E 3.0 to create misleading or false images that could spread misinformation or deceive people.

Example:
Unethical Prompt: "An image of a historical event that did not happen." *Ethical Prompt:* "An artistic representation of a well-documented historical event."

Ensuring accuracy and honesty in the images you generate helps prevent the spread of misinformation.

4. Promoting Positive Social Impact

Principle:
Use DALL·E 3.0 to create images that have a positive social impact, such as promoting education, awareness, and inclusivity.

Example:
Prompt: "An illustration showing diverse people working together to clean up a beach."

Creating images that inspire positive action and social good contributes to a better community and world.

Responsible Practices

1. Transparency and Disclosure

Practice:
Clearly disclose when an image is AI-generated, especially in contexts where viewers might assume the image is real.

Example:
In a social media post featuring an AI-generated image, include a note like "This image was created using AI technology."

Transparency helps maintain trust and allows viewers to make informed judgments about the content they are viewing.

2. Attribution and Credit

Practice:
When using AI-generated images, give credit to the technology and creators behind the AI.

Example:
Include a statement such as "Image created with DALL·E 3.0 by OpenAI" in any publications or presentations featuring the generated image.

Attribution acknowledges the technology's role and the work of those who developed it.

3. Monitoring and Moderation

Practice:
Regularly monitor the outputs generated by DALL·E 3.0 and apply moderation to ensure they align with ethical guidelines and standards.

Example:
Review generated images for any inappropriate or harmful content before sharing or publishing them.

Active moderation helps prevent unintended misuse and ensures that all content is appropriate and ethical.

4. Engaging with Diverse Perspectives

Practice:
Incorporate diverse perspectives and feedback when using DALL·E 3.0, particularly when creating content that represents different cultures or communities.

Example:
When generating images that depict cultural traditions, consult

with individuals from those cultures to ensure accuracy and sensitivity.

Engaging with diverse perspectives helps create more respectful and authentic representations.

5. Continuous Learning and Adaptation

Practice:
Stay informed about the ethical implications of AI technology and continuously adapt your practices to align with evolving standards and best practices.

Example:
Participate in discussions and training on AI ethics to stay updated on the latest guidelines and ethical considerations.

Ongoing learning ensures that your use of AI technology remains responsible and up-to-date.

Practical Examples of Ethical Use

Example 1: Educational Content *Ethical Use:* Creating detailed and accurate illustrations for educational materials, such as diagrams of scientific concepts or historical events.

Example 2: Inclusive Marketing *Ethical Use:* Generating marketing images that reflect diversity and inclusivity, such as advertisements featuring people of different ages, ethnicities, and abilities working together.

Example 3: Positive Advocacy *Ethical Use:* Designing images for advocacy campaigns that promote environmental conservation, social justice, or public health, such as visuals encouraging recycling or vaccination.

<u>Ethical Considerations In AI-Generated Art</u>

AI-generated art, such as images created using DALL·E 3.0, offers exciting possibilities for creativity and innovation. However, it also raises important ethical considerations that must be addressed to ensure responsible use.

Key Ethical Considerations

1. Intellectual Property and Copyright

Consideration:
Respect for intellectual property and copyright laws is crucial in AI-generated art. Using AI to generate images based on copyrighted material without permission can lead to legal and ethical issues.

Example:
Unethical Use: Generating an image closely resembling a famous copyrighted painting and selling it as an original piece. *Ethical Use:* Creating an entirely new artwork inspired by general themes or styles from different artists without copying specific elements.

Respecting the boundaries of intellectual property ensures that the rights of original creators are upheld.

2. Authenticity and Transparency

Consideration:
It is important to be transparent about the use of AI in creating art. Viewers and consumers should know when they are looking at AI-generated work.

Example:
Unethical Use: Presenting AI-generated art as a purely human creation without disclosing the involvement of AI. *Ethical Use:*

Clearly stating in the artwork's description or title that it was created using AI, such as "Generated with DALL·E 3.0."

Transparency builds trust and allows for an honest appreciation of AI's role in the creative process.

3. Cultural Sensitivity and Appropriation

Consideration:
AI-generated art should be culturally sensitive and avoid appropriation. Using cultural symbols, attire, or themes without proper understanding or respect can be offensive.

Example:
Unethical Use: Generating images that depict sacred symbols or traditional attire from a culture in a disrespectful or trivializing manner. *Ethical Use:* Engaging with cultural representatives to ensure respectful and accurate representation when incorporating cultural elements into AI-generated art.

Being mindful of cultural sensitivity fosters respect and inclusivity.

4. Ethical Representation and Diversity

Consideration:
AI-generated art should strive for diverse and fair representation of different groups, avoiding stereotypes or biased depictions.

Example:
Unethical Use: Creating stereotypical images that reinforce harmful biases or exclude certain groups. *Ethical Use:* Intentionally generating diverse images that positively represent various ethnicities, genders, ages, and abilities.

Promoting diversity in AI-generated art supports social equity and representation.

5. Avoiding Harmful Content

Consideration:
AI-generated art should not be used to create or propagate harmful content, including violence, hate speech, or explicit material.

Example:
Unethical Use: Generating graphic or violent images that could cause distress or incite violence. *Ethical Use:* Focusing on creating art that is positive, educational, or enriching, avoiding content that could be harmful or offensive.

Ensuring the content is safe and appropriate contributes to the positive impact of AI-generated art.

Practical Examples of Ethical Considerations

Example 1: Intellectual Property and Copyright *Ethical Approach:* An artist uses DALL·E 3.0 to create a new artwork inspired by the impressionist style but ensures the composition, subject, and elements are original and not directly copied from any existing works.

Example 2: Authenticity and Transparency *Ethical Approach:* A designer creates a digital artwork using DALL·E 3.0 and includes a disclaimer in the artwork's description, such as "This piece was created using AI technology with DALL·E 3.0."

Example 3: Cultural Sensitivity and Appropriation *Ethical Approach:* When generating art that includes cultural elements, the artist consults with members of that culture to ensure the representation is accurate and respectful, such as creating an image of a traditional Japanese tea ceremony with guidance from Japanese cultural experts.

Example 4: Ethical Representation and Diversity *Ethical Approach:* A project aims to create portraits of people from around the world using DALL·E 3.0. The team ensures a wide range of ethnicities, ages, and genders are represented, avoiding stereotypes and promoting inclusivity.

Example 5: Avoiding Harmful Content *Ethical Approach:* A content creator uses DALL·E 3.0 to generate images for a children's book. They carefully craft prompts to ensure the images are child-friendly, positive, and educational, steering clear of any violent or inappropriate content.

Best Practices for Ethical AI-Generated Art

1. Informed Consent and Collaboration

Practice:
When incorporating elements related to specific cultures or communities, seek informed consent and collaborate with representatives from those groups.

Example:
Collaborate with Indigenous artists when creating AI-generated art that includes Indigenous symbols or motifs to ensure authenticity and respect.

2. Regular Ethical Reviews

Practice:
Conduct regular reviews of your AI-generated art projects to ensure they adhere to ethical guidelines and adjust practices as needed.

Example:
Set up an ethics review panel to periodically evaluate the content produced and provide feedback on ethical considerations.

3. Public Engagement and Education

Practice:
Engage the public in discussions about AI-generated art and

educate them on the technology, its benefits, and its ethical implications.

Example:
Host workshops or webinars on AI in art, discussing how tools like DALL·E 3.0 work, their creative potential, and the importance of ethical use.

4. Continuous Learning and Adaptation

Practice:
Stay informed about developments in AI ethics and continuously adapt your practices to reflect the latest standards and best practices.

Example:
Attend conferences, read up-to-date literature on AI ethics, and participate in online courses to keep your knowledge current and your practices responsible.

Ethical considerations in AI-generated art are crucial for ensuring that this powerful technology is used responsibly and constructively. By respecting intellectual property, being transparent about AI use, practicing cultural sensitivity, promoting diversity, and avoiding harmful content, creators can harness the potential of AI like DALL·E 3.0 to produce art that is not only innovative but also ethical. Implementing best practices such as informed consent, regular ethical reviews, public engagement, and continuous learning will further support the responsible use of AI in the art world. By prioritizing ethics, we can ensure that AI-generated art contributes positively to society and culture.

Respecting Copyright and Intellectual Property

Respecting copyright and intellectual property is a fundamental aspect of ethical behavior when using AI tools like

DALL·E 3.0. Copyright laws are designed to protect the rights of creators and ensure they receive recognition and compensation for their work. Misuse of AI to generate images that violate these rights can lead to legal issues and ethical concerns.

Key Principles of Respecting Copyright and Intellectual Property

1. Understanding Copyright Laws

Principle:
Familiarize yourself with the basics of copyright laws and how they apply to both traditional and AI-generated art. This knowledge helps avoid unintentional violations.

Example:
Recognize that using a famous painting as a direct template for AI-generated art without permission is a copyright violation. Instead, create original compositions inspired by general artistic styles.

2. Avoiding Direct Replication

Principle:
Avoid using AI to directly replicate or create derivative works from copyrighted material without explicit permission from the original creator.

Example:
Unethical Use: Generating an image that closely mimics a well-known cartoon character. *Ethical Use:* Designing an entirely new character with unique features and personality traits that do not infringe on existing intellectual property.

3. Seeking Permission and Licensing

Principle:
Obtain proper licensing or permission when you intend to use copyrighted material as part of your AI-generated art.

Example:
If you want to generate art based on a popular book's illustrations, seek permission from the publisher or author to use their work legally and ethically.

4. Citing Sources and Providing Attribution

Principle:
When your AI-generated art is inspired by or incorporates elements from other works, give appropriate credit to the original creators.

Example:
Ethical Use: "This artwork was inspired by the Impressionist style of Claude Monet."

By citing sources, you acknowledge the original creators' contributions and maintain transparency about your creative process.

5. Creating Original Content

Principle:
Focus on creating original content with AI, using it as a tool to enhance creativity rather than to replicate existing works.

Example:
Ethical Approach: Using DALL·E 3.0 to generate a unique landscape painting based on a detailed description of an imaginary place, rather than copying a famous landscape.

Practical Examples of Respecting Copyright and Intellectual Property

Example 1: Original Artwork Creation *Scenario:* An artist uses DALL·E 3.0 to generate a series of landscape paintings. *Ethical Approach:* The artist describes original scenes, such as "a fantasy forest with bioluminescent plants and a glowing river," ensuring that the generated images are unique and not derivative of existing works.

Example 2: Licensed Use of Source Material *Scenario:* A designer wants to create AI-generated posters featuring characters from a popular movie. *Ethical Approach:* The designer contacts the movie studio to obtain the necessary licenses and permissions to use the characters, ensuring all usage is legal and compensated.

Example 3: Attribution in AI-Generated Art *Scenario:* A digital artist creates AI-generated art inspired by the Cubist movement. *Ethical Approach:* The artist includes a note with each piece, such as "Inspired by the Cubist art of Pablo Picasso," providing proper attribution and context.

Example 4: Avoiding Infringement *Scenario:* A content creator uses DALL·E 3.0 to generate book illustrations. *Unethical Use:* Generating images that replicate iconic illustrations from another book series. *Ethical Approach:* Creating entirely new illustrations based on original characters and scenes described in the new book, ensuring no infringement on existing works.

Example 5: Educational and Non-Commercial Use *Scenario:* A teacher uses DALL·E 3.0 to create educational materials for a classroom. *Ethical Approach:* The teacher ensures all generated images are original or based on public domain works and provides proper attribution where necessary, especially if using any elements from existing educational resources.

Best Practices for Respecting Copyright and Intellectual Property

1. Educate Yourself and Others

Practice:
Learn about copyright laws relevant to your region and educate others who work with you about these principles.

Example:
Attend workshops on copyright laws for artists and designers, and share this knowledge with your team to ensure everyone adheres to ethical practices.

2. Use Public Domain and Creative Commons Resources

Practice:
Utilize public domain works or those under Creative Commons licenses for inspiration, ensuring compliance with the terms of use.

Example:
Incorporate elements from public domain art in your AI-generated works, or use Creative Commons-licensed images with proper attribution as specified by the license.

3. Maintain Clear Documentation

Practice:
Document the sources of inspiration and the steps taken to ensure originality and compliance with copyright laws in your creative process.

Example:
Keep a log of all references and permissions obtained for each project, detailing how each source was used or incorporated into the final AI-generated art.

4. Regularly Review and Update Practices

Practice:
Periodically review and update your practices to ensure they remain compliant with current copyright laws and ethical standards.

Example:
Conduct annual reviews of your creative processes and ethical

guidelines, making adjustments based on new developments in copyright law or industry best practices.

Respecting copyright and intellectual property is a critical component of ethical behavior when using AI tools like DALL·E 3.0. By understanding copyright laws, avoiding direct replication, seeking permission and licensing, citing sources, and focusing on creating original content, you can ensure that your use of AI-generated art is responsible and ethical. Implementing best practices such as educating yourself and others, using public domain and Creative Commons resources, maintaining clear documentation, and regularly reviewing and updating practices further supports the ethical use of AI in art. By prioritizing respect for intellectual property, you contribute to a fair and sustainable creative ecosystem

Promoting Inclusivity and Diversity In Prompts

Promoting inclusivity and diversity in AI-generated art is essential for creating a respectful and representative body of work. When using tools like DALL·E 3.0, it is important to consciously incorporate diverse perspectives and ensure fair representation of different groups.

Key Principles of Inclusivity and Diversity

1. Representing Different Cultures and Ethnicities

Principle:
Ensure that your prompts include a wide range of cultures and ethnicities, avoiding stereotypes and promoting accurate and respectful representations.

Example:
Inclusive Prompt: "A celebration of Diwali with families lighting lamps, sharing sweets, and enjoying fireworks in a beautifully

decorated courtyard." *Diverse Prompt:* "A traditional Japanese tea ceremony with participants in kimonos, a serene garden setting, and a tea house in the background."

By including diverse cultural contexts, you foster a richer and more inclusive visual narrative.

2. Depicting Various Genders and Identities

Principle:
Incorporate diverse gender identities and expressions in your prompts, moving beyond traditional gender norms and roles.

Example:
Inclusive Prompt: "A group of friends at a café, including men, women, and non-binary individuals, all engaged in animated conversation." *Diverse Prompt:* "A woman wearing a business suit giving a presentation in a corporate boardroom, with colleagues of various genders and backgrounds."

This approach ensures that different gender identities are represented and respected.

3. Showcasing Different Ages and Abilities

Principle:
Include people of different ages and abilities in your prompts, highlighting the contributions and presence of all groups.

Example:
Inclusive Prompt: "A community park with children playing, elderly people walking, and a person in a wheelchair enjoying the scenery." *Diverse Prompt:* "A university classroom with students of various ages, including a mature student, all engaged in a collaborative project."

Promoting age and ability diversity enriches the representation of human experiences.

4. Avoiding Stereotypes and Bias

Principle:

Craft prompts that avoid reinforcing stereotypes or biases, focusing instead on authentic and varied representations.

Example:

Biased Prompt: "A scientist working in a lab, assumed to be a male." *Inclusive Prompt:* "A diverse team of scientists, including women and men of different ethnic backgrounds, working together in a high-tech laboratory."

By challenging stereotypes, you create a more balanced and fair depiction of different roles and professions.

Practical Strategies for Promoting Inclusivity and Diversity

1. Thoughtful Language and Descriptions

Strategy:

Use thoughtful and inclusive language in your prompts to ensure fair representation.

Example:

Basic Prompt: "A family at dinner." *Inclusive Prompt:* "A multicultural family enjoying a meal together, with dishes from various cuisines on the table."

2. Including Diverse Settings and Contexts

Strategy:

Set your scenes in a variety of cultural and social contexts to reflect the diversity of human experiences.

Example:

Basic Prompt: "A city street." *Diverse Prompt:* "A vibrant city street with a multicultural crowd, including a food festival with stalls from different countries and people in traditional attire."

3. Highlighting Underrepresented Groups

Strategy:
Make a conscious effort to highlight groups that are often underrepresented in media and art.

Example:
Basic Prompt: "A group of musicians." *Inclusive Prompt:* "A diverse band with musicians of different ethnicities, genders, and ages, including a visually impaired pianist."

4. Consulting and Collaborating

Strategy:
Collaborate with people from different backgrounds to ensure accurate and respectful representations.

Example:
When creating prompts related to a specific culture, seek input from individuals who belong to that culture to ensure authenticity and respect.

5. Regular Review and Feedback

Strategy:
Regularly review your work and seek feedback to identify areas for improvement in inclusivity and diversity.

Example:
Create a checklist for reviewing prompts to ensure they include diverse and inclusive elements, and seek feedback from diverse groups to refine your approach.

Examples of Inclusive and Diverse Prompts

Example 1: Diverse Professions *Scenario:* Creating prompts for professional settings. *Inclusive Prompt:* "A team meeting in an office, including a diverse group of professionals with different ethnic backgrounds, genders, and ages, collaborating on a project."

Example 2: Inclusive Recreational Activities *Scenario:* Generating images of leisure activities. *Inclusive Prompt:* "A beach scene with people of various body types, ages, and abilities, including a person in a wheelchair playing beach volleyball."

Example 3: Cultural Celebrations *Scenario:* Depicting cultural events. *Inclusive Prompt:* "A multicultural festival with traditional dances, food stalls, and attire from around the world, celebrating unity in diversity."

Example 4: Family Dynamics *Scenario:* Illustrating family life. *Inclusive Prompt:* "A family portrait with a multigenerational, multicultural family, including grandparents, parents, children, and a pet, all smiling together in a park."

Example 5: Academic Environments *Scenario:* Visualizing educational settings. *Inclusive Prompt:* "A diverse group of students in a university library, including international students and those with visible disabilities, all studying and interacting."

Best Practices for Promoting Inclusivity and Diversity

1. Educate Yourself and Others

Practice:
Continuously educate yourself and your team about the importance of inclusivity and diversity, and integrate these values into your work.

Example:
Attend workshops and training sessions on diversity and inclusion, and share insights with your team to promote a more inclusive creative process.

2. Use Inclusive Reference Materials

Practice:
Incorporate a wide range of reference materials that reflect diverse perspectives and experiences.

Example:
Use reference images and texts that include diverse cultures, body types, genders, and abilities to inform your prompts and ensure they are inclusive.

3. Foster an Inclusive Creative Environment

Practice:
Encourage an inclusive and respectful environment in your creative process, where all team members feel valued and heard.

Example:
Create an open forum for team members to share their ideas and experiences related to diversity, and integrate their feedback into your work.

4. Continuously Assess and Improve

Practice:
Regularly assess your work for inclusivity and diversity, and make improvements based on feedback and new insights.

Example:
Conduct periodic reviews of your prompts and generated images to ensure they continue to meet high standards of inclusivity and diversity.

Promoting inclusivity and diversity in AI-generated art is essential for creating respectful, accurate, and representative content. By representing different cultures, ethnicities, genders, ages, and abilities, and avoiding stereotypes and biases, you can ensure that your work reflects the richness and variety of human experiences. Implementing strategies such as using thoughtful language, including diverse settings, highlighting underrepresented groups, consulting with diverse individuals, and regularly reviewing your work helps foster inclusivity and diversity in your creative process. Through continuous education, the use of inclusive reference materials, fostering an inclusive environment, and ongoing assessment, you can ensure that your AI-generated art contributes positively to a more inclusive and diverse world.

Conclusion

Ethics and responsible use are paramount when working with AI tools like DALL·E 3.0. By adhering to principles such as avoiding harmful content, respecting privacy, avoiding misinformation, and promoting positive social impact, you can ensure that your use of the technology is ethical and constructive. Implementing responsible practices such as transparency, attribution, moderation, engaging with diverse perspectives, and continuous learning further enhances the integrity and positive impact of your work. By prioritizing ethics and responsibility, you contribute to the beneficial and respectful use of AI technology in society.

Chapter 9: Tools and Resources

Using the right tools and resources can significantly enhance the quality and effectiveness of your work with AI-generated art. These tools and resources range from software applications and platforms to educational materials and communities that support the creative process.

Essential Tools for AI-Generated Art

1. AI Image Generation Platforms

Description:
AI image generation platforms like DALL·E 3.0 enable users to create images from textual descriptions. These platforms are the core tools for generating and experimenting with AI art.

Example:
Using DALL·E 3.0, you can input a prompt such as "A futuristic cityscape with flying cars and neon lights" to generate a detailed image that matches the description.

2. Graphic Design Software

Description:
Graphic design software allows you to refine and enhance AI-generated images, add text, and combine multiple images. Tools like Adobe Photoshop, GIMP, and Canva are widely used.

Example:
After generating an image of a "medieval castle," you can use Adobe Photoshop to adjust the lighting, add text labels, and blend the image with other elements to create a complete scene.

3. Digital Drawing Tablets

Description:

Digital drawing tablets provide a hands-on way to refine AI-generated art by adding hand-drawn elements and making detailed adjustments.

Example:

Using a Wacom tablet, you can enhance the fine details of an AI-generated "forest landscape," adding intricate features like leaves and textures manually.

4. Image Editing and Enhancement Tools

Description:

These tools, such as Lightroom and Snapseed, help in fine-tuning the colors, contrast, and sharpness of AI-generated images to achieve the desired aesthetic quality.

Example:

Enhance an AI-generated "sunset over a beach" image using Lightroom to adjust the warmth and saturation, bringing out the vivid colors of the sunset.

5. 3D Modeling Software

Description:

For more advanced projects, 3D modeling software like Blender or SketchUp can be used to create three-dimensional models based on AI-generated images.

Example:

Generate a 2D concept of a "futuristic vehicle" using DALL·E 3.0, then use Blender to create a detailed 3D model that can be animated or further refined.

Valuable Resources for AI-Generated Art

1. Online Tutorials and Courses

Description:
Educational platforms offer tutorials and courses on AI art, graphic design, and digital illustration. These resources help users develop their skills and understand best practices.

Example:
Platforms like Coursera and Udemy offer courses on AI in art, teaching how to use tools like DALL·E 3.0 effectively and how to integrate AI-generated images into creative projects.

2. Digital Art Communities

Description:
Online communities and forums provide a space for artists to share their work, seek feedback, and collaborate on projects. These communities often include professional and amateur artists alike.

Example:
Joining a community like DeviantArt or ArtStation allows you to showcase your AI-generated art, receive constructive critiques, and network with other artists.

3. Reference Image Libraries

Description:
Libraries of reference images, such as Unsplash, Pixabay, and Pexels, provide inspiration and reference material for creating and refining AI-generated art.

Example:
When generating an image of a "tropical rainforest," you can use reference images from Unsplash to guide the details and ensure accuracy in the portrayal of plant species and environments.

4. Creative Commons Resources

Description:
Creative Commons resources offer a range of images and materials

that can be used freely under specific licensing conditions, providing a rich source of inspiration and elements for your projects.

Example:
Incorporate Creative Commons-licensed textures and backgrounds into your AI-generated art, ensuring compliance with the licensing terms.

5. AI Art and Design Blogs

Description:
Blogs and websites dedicated to AI art and design offer insights, tips, and the latest trends in the field. These resources keep you updated on new tools, techniques, and ethical considerations.

Example:
Following blogs like AIArtists.org provides you with the latest developments in AI art, including new tools, success stories, and tutorials on improving your AI-generated creations.

Practical Examples of Using Tools and Resources

Example 1: Enhancing an AI-Generated Image *Scenario:* You have generated an image of a "space station orbiting Earth" using DALL·E 3.0. *Process:* Use Adobe Photoshop to enhance the image by adjusting the brightness and contrast, adding text annotations for different sections of the space station, and blending in a background image of Earth from a Creative Commons source.

Example 2: Creating a Digital Illustration *Scenario:* You want to create a detailed digital illustration of a "mythical creature in a fantasy forest." *Process:* Generate the base image using DALL·E 3.0, then refine and add details using a digital drawing tablet with software like Procreate. Enhance colors and textures with Lightroom to achieve the final look.

Example 3: Developing a 3D Model *Scenario:* You have an AI-generated concept of a "futuristic building." *Process:* Use the generated image as a reference in SketchUp to build a detailed 3D model, adding structural details and exploring different architectural styles.

Example 4: Learning and Skill Development *Scenario:* You want to improve your skills in using AI tools for art. *Process:* Enroll in a course on Coursera about AI in art, participate in online workshops, and practice by creating and sharing your work in digital art communities like ArtStation for feedback.

Example 5: Collaborating with Other Artists *Scenario:* You are working on a collaborative art project. *Process:* Use a platform like DeviantArt to connect with other artists, share your AI-generated concepts, and integrate their feedback and contributions into a cohesive final piece.

Best Practices for Using Tools and Resources

1. Continuous Learning and Adaptation

Practice:
Stay updated with the latest tools, techniques, and trends in AI-generated art by engaging with educational resources and professional development opportunities.

Example:
Regularly attend webinars, read industry blogs, and participate in online courses to keep your skills sharp and your knowledge current.

2. Ethical Use of Resources

Practice:
Ensure all resources and tools are used ethically, respecting copyright laws and licensing agreements.

Example:
Always check the licensing terms of Creative Commons images before using them in your projects, and give proper attribution when required.

3. Engaging with Communities

Practice:
Actively participate in digital art communities to share your work, seek feedback, and collaborate with other artists.

Example:
Post your AI-generated art on forums like Reddit's r/DigitalArt, engage in discussions, and incorporate constructive feedback to improve your work.

4. Leveraging a Variety of Tools

Practice:
Utilize a combination of AI tools, graphic design software, and reference materials to create comprehensive and polished final products.

Example:
Combine the capabilities of DALL·E 3.0 with Adobe Photoshop for image refinement and Blender for 3D modeling to create a multi-dimensional art piece.

5. Documenting Your Process

Practice:
Keep detailed records of your creative process, including the tools and resources used, to track your progress and refine your techniques.

Example:
Maintain a digital journal of your projects, noting each step from

prompt generation with DALL·E 3.0 to final enhancements in graphic design software.

Software And Platforms for Prompt Writing

Crafting effective prompts is crucial for generating high-quality images with AI tools like DALL·E 3.0. Several software and platforms can aid in writing and refining prompts, ensuring clarity, creativity, and specificity.

Key Software and Platforms for Prompt Writing

1. Text Editors

Description:
Basic text editors, such as Microsoft Word, Google Docs, and Notepad, are essential for drafting, editing, and organizing your prompts. They provide the fundamental tools needed for writing clear and structured text.

Example:
Using Google Docs, you can draft a prompt like "A tranquil forest clearing at dawn, with mist rising from a small pond and rays of sunlight filtering through the trees." The document's collaborative features allow you to share and receive feedback from others in real-time.

2. Grammar and Style Checkers

Description:
Grammar and style checkers like Grammarly and Hemingway Editor help ensure your prompts are clear, grammatically correct, and stylistically effective. These tools highlight errors and suggest improvements.

Example:
After writing a prompt in Microsoft Word, run it through

Grammarly to check for clarity and grammar. For instance, "A bustling city market with vendors, shoppers, and street performers" might be refined to "A bustling city market with lively vendors, eager shoppers, and captivating street performers."

3. Creative Writing Platforms

Description:
Creative writing platforms such as Scrivener and Ulysses are designed to help writers organize their ideas and craft detailed narratives. These platforms are particularly useful for developing complex prompts with multiple elements.

Example:
Using Scrivener, you can create a detailed prompt for a fantasy scene: "A majestic dragon perched on a rocky cliff overlooking a medieval castle, with knights preparing for battle in the valley below." Scrivener's organizational features allow you to break down the prompt into smaller components and refine each part.

4. Mind Mapping Tools

Description:
Mind mapping tools like MindMeister and XMind help visualize and organize your ideas. These tools are beneficial for brainstorming and structuring prompts, ensuring all necessary elements are included.

Example:
In MindMeister, you can create a mind map for a prompt about a futuristic city. Start with the central idea "Futuristic City" and branch out to include details like "hovering cars," "neon lights," "robotic citizens," and "glass skyscrapers." This visualization helps ensure a comprehensive and detailed prompt.

5. AI Writing Assistants

Description:
AI writing assistants like ChatGPT can help generate ideas, refine prompts, and suggest improvements. These tools use natural language processing to assist in crafting effective and creative prompts.

Example:
Using an AI writing assistant, you might start with a basic idea like "a space station." The assistant could help refine this to "A bustling space station orbiting Earth, with astronauts floating in zero gravity and large windows offering views of distant galaxies."

6. Collaboration Platforms

Description:
Collaboration platforms such as Slack, Trello, and Asana facilitate teamwork by allowing multiple users to contribute to and refine prompts. These tools are ideal for group projects where input from various stakeholders is needed.

Example:
On Trello, create a board for a project involving AI-generated art. Add cards for different prompts, such as "Enchanted forest," "Urban jungle," and "Underwater city." Team members can add details, suggest improvements, and move cards through stages of refinement.

Practical Examples of Using Software and Platforms for Prompt Writing

Example 1: Drafting and Refining Prompts *Scenario:* Writing a prompt for a serene garden scene. *Process:*

1. Draft the prompt in Google Docs: "A peaceful garden with colorful flowers and a bubbling fountain."

2. Use Grammarly to check for clarity and correctness, refining it to: "A peaceful garden filled with vibrant flowers and a gently bubbling fountain, with butterflies fluttering around."

Example 2: Organizing Complex Prompts *Scenario:* Developing a multi-element prompt for a fantasy battle scene. *Process:*

1. Use Scrivener to break down the prompt into sections: "Setting," "Characters," and "Action."

2. Write detailed descriptions for each section, such as "Setting: A dark, enchanted forest under a full moon" and "Characters: Brave knights and mythical creatures preparing for an epic battle."

Example 3: Brainstorming and Structuring Ideas *Scenario:* Creating a prompt for a futuristic city. *Process:*

1. Start a mind map in MindMeister with the central idea "Futuristic City."

2. Branch out to include specific elements like "hovering cars," "neon lights," "robotic citizens," and "glass skyscrapers."

3. Use the mind map to draft a comprehensive prompt in a text editor: "A vibrant futuristic city with neon-lit streets, hovering cars zipping through the air, robotic citizens interacting, and towering glass skyscrapers."

Example 4: Enhancing Creativity with AI Assistance *Scenario:* Generating ideas for a magical underwater kingdom. *Process:*

1. Describe the basic concept to an AI writing assistant: "a magical underwater kingdom."

2. Use the assistant's suggestions to refine the prompt: "A magical underwater kingdom with glowing coral reefs, mermaids swimming gracefully, and a grand palace made of pearls and shells."

Example 5: Collaborative Prompt Development *Scenario:* Developing prompts for a series of educational illustrations. *Process:*

1. Set up a Trello board with cards for each illustration topic, such as "Photosynthesis," "Water Cycle," and "Human Anatomy."

2. Team members add details and refine prompts collaboratively, moving cards through stages of brainstorming, drafting, and final review.

Best Practices for Using Software and Platforms for Prompt Writing

1. Consistent Organization and Documentation

Practice:
Keep all drafts, revisions, and feedback organized and well-documented to track the development process.

Example:
Maintain a dedicated folder in Google Drive for each project, with subfolders for initial drafts, revisions, and final prompts.

2. Leveraging Collaborative Tools

Practice:
Use collaboration tools to gather diverse input and perspectives, enhancing the richness and creativity of your prompts.

Example:

Regularly schedule brainstorming sessions on Slack or Zoom, where team members can discuss and refine prompt ideas.

3. Regularly Reviewing and Refining Prompts

Practice:

Periodically review and refine your prompts to ensure clarity, specificity, and creativity.

Example:

Set aside time each week to revisit and polish prompts, incorporating any new ideas or improvements suggested by team members or AI writing assistants.

4. Utilizing Feedback Effectively

Practice:

Actively seek and incorporate feedback from peers, mentors, or AI tools to improve the quality of your prompts.

Example:

After drafting a prompt, share it with colleagues via Google Docs and invite comments and suggestions for improvement.

5. Balancing Creativity with Clarity

Practice:

Ensure that while your prompts are creative and imaginative, they remain clear and easy to understand for the AI tool.

Example:

Use descriptive language to paint a vivid picture but avoid overly complex or ambiguous terms that might confuse the AI.

Effective prompt writing is crucial for generating high-quality images with AI tools like DALL·E 3.0. Utilizing software and platforms such as text editors, grammar and style checkers, creative writing platforms, mind mapping tools, AI writing assistants, and collaboration platforms can significantly enhance the quality and creativity of your prompts. By following best practices for organization, collaboration, regular review, effective use of feedback, and balancing creativity with clarity, you can craft detailed and imaginative prompts that lead to compelling and accurate AI-generated art.

<u>Online Communities and Forums</u>

Online communities and forums play a vital role in the development and refinement of AI-generated art. These platforms offer spaces for artists, developers, and enthusiasts to share their work, exchange ideas, seek feedback, and collaborate on projects. Engaging with these communities can significantly enhance your skills, provide inspiration, and keep you updated on the latest trends and techniques.

Key Online Communities and Forums

1. ArtStation

Description:
ArtStation is a popular platform for professional artists to showcase their work, including AI-generated art. It offers a range of features such as portfolios, tutorials, and a marketplace.

Example:
Create a profile on ArtStation to showcase your AI-generated images, such as a portfolio of futuristic cityscapes created with DALL·E 3.0. Engage with other artists by commenting on their work and participating in challenges or contests.

2. DeviantArt

Description:

DeviantArt is a large online community for artists of all levels. It supports a wide variety of art forms, including digital art, traditional art, and AI-generated art.

Example:

Join groups focused on AI art within DeviantArt to share your creations, such as a series of AI-generated fantasy characters. Participate in group discussions and receive feedback from other members to improve your prompts and techniques.

3. Reddit

Description:

Reddit hosts numerous subreddits dedicated to different aspects of AI, digital art, and creative technologies. These forums provide a space for sharing work, asking questions, and discussing trends.

Example:

Participate in subreddits like r/DigitalArt and r/AIArt by posting your latest AI-generated images and seeking constructive criticism. Join discussions on topics such as ethical considerations in AI art or new features in DALL·E 3.0.

4. Discord

Description:

Discord is a communication platform with servers dedicated to various interests, including AI and digital art. These servers offer real-time chat, voice channels, and collaborative tools.

Example:

Join a Discord server dedicated to AI art to collaborate on projects, such as a community-driven anthology of AI-generated illustrations. Use voice channels for brainstorming sessions and text channels to share progress and receive feedback.

5. Facebook Groups

Description:
Facebook groups offer communities focused on specific interests and can be a valuable resource for AI artists looking to connect with others and share their work.

Example:
Join a Facebook group focused on AI-generated art to post your latest creations, such as AI-enhanced photo manipulations. Engage in group discussions about techniques, tools, and industry news.

Practical Examples of Utilizing Online Communities and Forums

Example 1: Seeking Feedback and Improvement *Scenario:* You have created a series of AI-generated landscapes and want to improve their quality. *Process:* Post the images in an ArtStation group dedicated to digital landscapes. Ask for specific feedback on aspects like composition, color balance, and detail. Use the feedback to refine your prompts and generate improved images.

Example 2: Collaborating on a Project *Scenario:* You want to create a collaborative project involving AI-generated characters. *Process:* Join a relevant Discord server and propose your project idea in the general chat. Recruit members interested in contributing different elements, such as character design, background art, and story development. Use the server's collaboration tools to coordinate and share progress.

Example 3: Staying Updated with Trends *Scenario:* You want to stay informed about the latest developments in AI art. *Process:* Follow subreddits like r/AIArt and r/MachineLearning on Reddit. Participate in discussions about new tools, techniques, and ethical considerations. Share articles and tutorials you find useful, and engage with posts from other users to broaden your knowledge.

Example 4: Sharing Educational Resources *Scenario:* You have developed a new technique for refining AI-generated images. *Process:* Write a detailed tutorial and share it in a DeviantArt group dedicated to AI art. Include step-by-step instructions and examples of your work. Encourage other members to try the technique and provide feedback on their experiences.

Example 5: Building a Network *Scenario:* You want to connect with other AI artists and expand your professional network. *Process:* Join Facebook groups related to AI and digital art. Participate regularly by posting your work, commenting on others' posts, and joining group events like live streams or Q&A sessions. Build relationships with other members and explore potential collaborations.

Best Practices for Engaging with Online Communities and Forums

1. Be Active and Consistent

Practice:
Regularly participate in discussions, share your work, and provide feedback to others. Consistent engagement helps build your presence in the community and fosters meaningful connections.

Example:
Set aside time each week to post new work on DeviantArt, comment on other artists' pieces, and participate in community challenges or discussions.

2. Provide Constructive Feedback

Practice:
When giving feedback, be constructive and specific. Highlight what you like about the work and offer suggestions for improvement in a respectful manner.

Example:
On Reddit, when someone shares an AI-generated portrait, comment with, "I love the color palette and lighting! You might consider adding more texture to the background to enhance the depth."

3. Seek and Incorporate Feedback

Practice:
Be open to feedback and willing to make adjustments based on constructive criticism. This helps improve your skills and the quality of your work.

Example:
After receiving feedback on ArtStation about the lack of contrast in your AI-generated images, adjust your prompts and use image editing tools to enhance contrast and re-share the improved images.

4. Respect Community Guidelines

Practice:
Follow the rules and guidelines of each community. Respectful behavior and adherence to community standards foster a positive environment for all members.

Example:
On Discord, ensure your posts are in the correct channels, avoid spamming, and respect the server's guidelines regarding the content and interactions.

5. Share Knowledge and Resources

Practice:
Contribute to the community by sharing tutorials, resources, and insights. Helping others enhances the collective knowledge and strengthens the community.

Example:
Create a detailed tutorial on using DALL·E 3.0 for beginners and share it on a Facebook group, along with links to helpful resources and tools.

Engaging with online communities and forums is crucial for the development and refinement of AI-generated art. Platforms like ArtStation, DeviantArt, Reddit, Discord, and Facebook groups offer valuable spaces for sharing work, seeking feedback, collaborating on projects, and staying updated on trends. By being active and consistent, providing and seeking constructive feedback, respecting community guidelines, and sharing knowledge, you can make the most of these resources and enhance your skills and network in the AI art community. These practices ensure a supportive and dynamic environment for all members, fostering creativity and innovation in AI-generated art.

Recommended Reading and Further Learning

Continuing education and staying informed about the latest developments in AI-generated art are crucial for honing your skills and understanding the broader implications of this technology. Engaging with recommended reading and further learning resources can provide deeper insights into techniques, ethical considerations, and the future of AI in art.

Recommended Books

1. "Artificial Intelligence: A Guide for Thinking Humans"

Description:
This book offers a comprehensive overview of AI, its development, and its impact on various fields, including art. It provides a solid foundation for understanding the principles and applications of AI.

Example:

Reading this book can help you grasp the fundamental concepts of AI, enabling you to better understand how tools like DALL·E 3.0 function and how to use them effectively in your creative process.

2. "The Artist's Guide to GIMP: Creative Techniques for Photographers, Artists, and Designers"

Description:

This guide provides detailed instructions on using GIMP, a free and open-source image editing software. It covers various techniques that can be applied to refine and enhance AI-generated images.

Example:

Use the book's tutorials to learn how to adjust colors, add layers, and apply filters to your AI-generated art, improving the final quality and making it more professional.

3. "Deep Learning with Python"

Description:

This book introduces deep learning concepts using Python, a key programming language in AI development. It includes practical examples and exercises.

Example:

By working through this book, you can gain a deeper understanding of the algorithms behind AI tools and possibly develop custom applications or enhancements for AI-generated art.

Essential Articles and Research Papers

1. "The Future of Creativity: How AI is Changing the Art World"

Description:

This article explores the impact of AI on the art world, including how artists are using AI tools to push the boundaries of creativity and what the future might hold.

Example:
Reading this article can provide inspiration and context for how your work with AI-generated art fits into the larger movement within the art community.

2. "Ethical Considerations in AI Art"

Description:
This paper discusses the ethical implications of AI in art, including issues related to copyright, bias, and the role of the artist.

Example:
Understanding these ethical considerations can guide you in making responsible choices when creating and sharing AI-generated art, ensuring your work respects both legal and moral standards.

3. "Generative Adversarial Networks: A Primer"

Description:
This research paper explains the concept of Generative Adversarial Networks (GANs), a crucial technology behind many AI art tools, including how they work and their applications.

Example:
By familiarizing yourself with GANs, you can better understand the technical workings of tools like DALL·E 3.0 and potentially experiment with creating your own AI art models.

Online Courses and Tutorials

1. "Introduction to AI for Artists"

Description:
An online course designed to teach artists the basics of AI and how

to use AI tools to create art. It includes practical exercises and real-world examples.

Example:
Taking this course can help you get started with AI-generated art, learning how to craft effective prompts and use various tools to enhance your creative process.

2. "Mastering Digital Art with Photoshop"

Description:
This tutorial series covers advanced techniques in Photoshop, tailored for digital artists looking to refine their skills and improve their artwork.

Example:
By completing these tutorials, you can apply advanced editing techniques to your AI-generated images, such as creating realistic textures, enhancing lighting, and blending multiple elements seamlessly.

3. "Deep Learning Specialization"

Description:
A comprehensive course that covers deep learning from basics to advanced topics, including neural networks, convolutional networks, and sequence models.

Example:
For those interested in the technical side of AI, this specialization can provide the knowledge needed to understand and possibly develop AI tools, enhancing your ability to create and customize AI-generated art.

Additional Resources

1. AI Art Blogs and Websites

Description:
Blogs and websites dedicated to AI art offer a wealth of information, including tutorials, news, and interviews with artists who use AI.

Example:
Following a blog dedicated to AI art can keep you updated on the latest tools, trends, and techniques, providing continuous learning and inspiration for your work.

2. Professional Associations and Conferences

Description:
Joining professional associations or attending conferences focused on AI and digital art can provide networking opportunities, access to exclusive resources, and insights from industry leaders.

Example:
Attending an AI art conference can help you connect with other professionals in the field, share your work, and learn about cutting-edge developments and best practices.

3. Online Communities and Forums

Description:
Engaging with online communities and forums allows you to share your work, seek feedback, and collaborate with others interested in AI-generated art.

Example:
Participating in discussions on platforms like Reddit or Discord can provide valuable feedback on your projects, help you troubleshoot issues, and inspire new ideas through community interaction.

Practical Tips for Using Recommended Reading and Further Learning Resources

1. Schedule Regular Learning Time

Practice:
Dedicate regular time each week to read books, articles, or take online courses. Consistent learning helps keep your skills sharp and up-to-date.

Example:
Set aside an hour every Sunday afternoon to read a chapter from "Deep Learning with Python" or watch a tutorial from "Introduction to AI for Artists."

2. Apply What You Learn

Practice:
Immediately apply new techniques or concepts learned from books, courses, or articles to your projects. Practical application reinforces learning.

Example:
After reading about color correction in "The Artist's Guide to GIMP," apply these techniques to refine the colors in your latest AI-generated landscape.

3. Engage with the Community

Practice:
Discuss what you've learned with peers in online communities and forums. Sharing insights and asking questions can deepen your understanding.

Example:
Post a summary of a new technique you learned from a course on Reddit, and ask for additional tips or feedback from the community.

4. Stay Open to New Ideas

Practice:
Remain open to new ideas and perspectives by regularly exploring diverse resources and engaging with different viewpoints.

Example:
Read articles from various sources about the ethical implications of AI in art, and participate in discussions to explore how these ideas apply to your work.

5. Document Your Learning Journey

Practice:
Keep a journal or digital record of what you've learned, including notes, key takeaways, and how you've applied the knowledge.

Example:
Create a document where you summarize each book, article, or course, noting key concepts and practical applications to refer back to as you continue to develop your skills.

Recommended reading and further learning are essential for anyone looking to excel in AI-generated art. Books on AI and digital art, articles and research papers on current trends and ethical considerations, online courses and tutorials on technical skills, and additional resources like blogs, professional associations, and online communities provide a wealth of knowledge and inspiration. By dedicating regular time to learning, applying new skills, engaging with the community, staying open to new ideas, and documenting your learning journey, you can continuously enhance your capabilities and stay at the forefront of the evolving field of AI-generated art.

Conclusion

Using the right tools and resources is essential for maximizing the potential of AI-generated art. Platforms like DALL·E 3.0, graphic design software, digital drawing tablets, image editing tools, and 3D modeling software provide the technical capabilities needed to create high-quality art. Educational resources, digital art communities, reference image libraries, Creative Commons resources, and AI art blogs support continuous learning and skill development. By adopting best practices such as continuous learning, ethical use, community engagement, leveraging diverse tools, and documenting your process, you can effectively utilize these tools and resources to create compelling and responsible AI-generated art.

Chapter 10: Future of AI Art and Prompt Writing

The future of AI art and prompt writing is poised to be a transformative period characterized by rapid technological advancements, evolving creative practices, and significant ethical considerations. As AI tools become more sophisticated, the capabilities for generating complex, high-quality art will expand, opening up new possibilities for artists and creators.

Technological Advancements

1. Improved AI Models

Future Development:
AI models will continue to improve in their ability to understand and generate detailed, contextually accurate images from complex prompts. This includes better handling of nuances, emotions, and intricate scenes.

Example:
Future iterations of AI tools like DALL·E might generate a prompt such as "A bustling cyberpunk marketplace at night with holographic advertisements and diverse characters interacting" with even greater detail, realism, and coherence, capturing subtle interactions and atmospheric elements.

2. Real-Time Feedback and Adjustment

Future Development:
AI systems will offer real-time feedback and adjustments during the prompt writing process, allowing creators to see immediate changes and refine their prompts on the fly.

Example:
While crafting a prompt, an integrated AI assistant could suggest improvements and show live previews of potential outputs, such as

adjusting "A serene mountain lake at dawn" to include "with mist rising from the water and a family of ducks swimming by," refining the image as you write.

3. Multimodal Capabilities

Future Development:
AI will increasingly integrate multimodal capabilities, allowing for seamless combination of text, image, audio, and video inputs and outputs.

Example:
A prompt like "A whimsical forest scene with a gentle breeze and birdsong" could generate not only a visual image but also an accompanying soundscape, creating a more immersive and multisensory artistic experience.

Evolving Creative Practices

1. Collaborative AI-Art Creation

Future Development:
Artists will collaborate more deeply with AI, using it as a creative partner rather than just a tool. This collaboration will blend human intuition and AI precision to create innovative art forms.

Example:
An artist working on a graphic novel might use AI to generate initial character designs and scene layouts, then refine these elements by hand, iterating between human and AI inputs to create a cohesive and dynamic story.

2. Personalized Art Generation

Future Development:
AI will enable highly personalized art creation, allowing individuals to generate art tailored to their specific preferences and contexts, whether for personal enjoyment or professional use.

Example:

A user might input their favorite colors, themes, and art styles into an AI system, which then generates personalized home decor pieces or unique digital wallpapers that match their tastes perfectly.

3. Interactive and Dynamic Art

Future Development:

AI will facilitate the creation of interactive and dynamic art that changes and evolves over time based on user interaction or environmental factors.

Example:

An AI-generated installation in a public space might adjust its visuals and sounds in response to the movement and noise levels of passersby, creating a living artwork that reacts to its surroundings.

Ethical Considerations

1. Bias and Representation

Future Development:

Efforts will intensify to address and mitigate biases in AI models, ensuring fair and inclusive representation in AI-generated art.

Example:

AI developers will implement robust measures to ensure that prompts like "A corporate boardroom with diverse leaders" accurately and positively represent people of different genders, ethnicities, and backgrounds, avoiding stereotypes and biases.

2. Intellectual Property and Authorship

Future Development:

The conversation around intellectual property and authorship of AI-generated art will evolve, establishing clearer guidelines and legal frameworks.

Example:
Legal frameworks might emerge to delineate the rights of artists who use AI tools, ensuring they retain creative ownership while also acknowledging the contributions of the AI systems involved.

3. Responsible Use and Misuse Prevention

Future Development:
There will be increased focus on preventing the misuse of AI-generated art, such as creating deepfakes or harmful content, through stricter regulations and ethical guidelines.

Example:
Developers and policymakers will work together to implement safeguards that prevent the generation of malicious content, such as images that could be used for misinformation or harassment, ensuring AI tools are used responsibly.

Practical Examples of Future Trends

Example 1: Advanced Prompt Writing *Scenario:* An artist wants to create a detailed fantasy landscape. *Future Process:* Using an advanced AI tool, they input a prompt like "A mystical forest with bioluminescent plants, ancient ruins, and a full moon casting a silver glow." The AI provides real-time feedback and suggestions, such as adding "a gentle stream with sparkling water and a mythical creature perched on a rock," refining the prompt to enhance the image.

Example 2: Collaborative AI Projects *Scenario:* A team of game developers is designing a new virtual world. *Future Process:* They use AI to generate various environmental assets and character designs based on detailed prompts. The AI assists in creating a coherent world by suggesting adjustments and integrating elements seamlessly, while human designers fine-tune the aesthetics and gameplay aspects.

Example 3: Ethical AI Use in Advertising *Scenario:* A company wants to create an inclusive advertising campaign. *Future Process:* The marketing team uses AI to generate images that reflect diverse demographics. The AI, equipped with bias-mitigation protocols, ensures that all generated content fairly represents different groups. The campaign showcases various settings, such as "A diverse group of friends enjoying a meal at a sunny outdoor café" and "A family of different backgrounds celebrating a holiday together."

Best Practices for Embracing the Future of AI Art and Prompt Writing

1. Continuous Learning and Adaptation

Practice:
Stay informed about the latest developments in AI art technology and ethical guidelines. Adapt your practices to incorporate new tools and techniques responsibly.

Example:
Regularly attend webinars, read industry publications, and participate in workshops to keep your skills and knowledge up-to-date.

2. Experimentation and Creativity

Practice:
Embrace experimentation with AI tools to discover new creative possibilities. Combine AI-generated elements with traditional techniques to push artistic boundaries.

Example:
Use AI to generate initial concepts for a series of paintings, then add hand-painted details and textures to create unique, hybrid artworks.

3. Ethical Responsibility

Practice:
Prioritize ethical considerations in all aspects of AI art creation. Ensure fair representation, respect intellectual property rights, and prevent misuse.

Example:
Before publishing an AI-generated piece, review it for potential biases and ensure it respects the cultural contexts and intellectual property of all referenced elements.

4. Collaborative Approaches

Practice:
Foster collaboration between AI developers, artists, and ethicists to create responsible and innovative AI art practices.

Example:
Join or form interdisciplinary teams that include AI engineers, artists, and ethical advisors to develop projects that leverage AI's potential while addressing ethical concerns.

5. Personalization and User Engagement

Practice:
Leverage AI's ability to personalize art to engage users more deeply. Create interactive experiences that adapt to user inputs and preferences.

Example:
Develop an interactive digital art exhibit where visitors can influence the art in real-time through their movements and choices, creating a personalized and dynamic experience.

Emerging Trends and Technologies

The field of AI art and prompt writing is rapidly evolving, driven by emerging trends and technologies that enhance creative possibilities and streamline the artistic process. These advancements promise to revolutionize how artists interact with AI, making the creation of complex and high-quality art more accessible and intuitive.

Emerging Trends

1. Generative Pre-trained Transformers (GPT) and Enhanced Language Models

Trend:
Enhanced language models like GPT-4 and beyond are becoming increasingly sophisticated, improving their ability to understand and generate complex, nuanced text. These models can create highly detailed and specific prompts that lead to better AI-generated art.

Example:
Using an advanced GPT model, an artist could input a simple idea like "an enchanted garden." The model might expand this into a detailed prompt: "A lush, enchanted garden filled with vibrant, oversized flowers, glowing mushrooms, and sparkling streams under a twilight sky, with fairies fluttering around."

2. Integration of Augmented Reality (AR) and Virtual Reality (VR)

Trend:
AI-generated art is increasingly being integrated with AR and VR technologies, creating immersive, interactive experiences that transcend traditional mediums.

Example:
A VR headset could transport users into a fully AI-generated world where they can explore a "futuristic city with floating buildings and neon-lit streets." This interactive environment allows users to

walk through the city, interact with AI-generated characters, and influence the environment through their actions.

3. Real-Time Collaboration Tools

Trend:
Real-time collaboration tools are becoming more advanced, enabling multiple users to work on AI-generated art projects simultaneously from different locations. These tools facilitate seamless collaboration and creativity.

Example:
Artists in different parts of the world could use a collaborative platform to work together on a digital mural. One artist might generate the background scene of "a peaceful beach at sunrise," while another adds detailed elements like "children building sandcastles" and "a pod of dolphins swimming offshore."

4. AI-Enhanced Creativity Assistants

Trend:
AI-enhanced creativity assistants are tools designed to support artists by providing suggestions, refinements, and creative enhancements in real-time as they work on their projects.

Example:
An artist using an AI creativity assistant could start with a basic sketch of "a dragon perched on a mountain peak." The assistant might suggest adding "fiery breath," "glowing eyes," and "a stormy sky" to enhance the dramatic effect. It could also offer color palette options and compositional adjustments.

5. Personalized AI Models

Trend:
Personalized AI models trained on individual artists' styles and

preferences are emerging, allowing for highly customized and unique outputs that align closely with the artist's vision.

Example:
An artist who frequently creates abstract landscapes could train a personalized AI model to generate scenes with their specific artistic style, such as "swirling colors and dynamic brush strokes," ensuring each AI-generated piece maintains their unique aesthetic.

6. Ethical and Bias-Mitigating AI

Trend:
There is a growing focus on developing AI models that actively mitigate biases and ensure ethical considerations are embedded in the art creation process.

Example:
An AI tool designed to generate images of people might include safeguards to ensure diverse and respectful representations. When given a prompt like "a group of professionals in a meeting," the AI ensures fair representation of different genders, ethnicities, and abilities, avoiding stereotypes.

Emerging Technologies

1. Neural Style Transfer Enhancements

Technology:
Neural style transfer, a technique that applies the stylistic elements of one image to another, is becoming more advanced, allowing for more precise and sophisticated blending of styles.

Example:
An artist could use neural style transfer to combine the style of Van Gogh's "Starry Night" with a modern cityscape, creating a unique fusion of classic and contemporary art.

2. 3D Generative Models

Technology:
3D generative models are being developed to create detailed three-dimensional objects and scenes from textual descriptions, expanding the possibilities for virtual environments, games, and digital art.

Example:
A game developer could use a 3D generative model to create an entire alien planet based on a prompt like "a rocky terrain with towering crystal formations and bioluminescent flora under a purple sky."

3. Generative Adversarial Networks (GANs) Improvements

Technology:
GANs are continuously improving, offering higher resolution and more realistic outputs. This technology is crucial for generating lifelike images and refining artistic details.

Example:
Using an advanced GAN, an artist could generate hyper-realistic portraits from prompts like "an elderly woman with kind eyes and a weathered face, wearing traditional clothing."

4. Automated Animation and Motion Capture

Technology:
AI tools that automate animation and motion capture are making it easier to bring static images to life, adding movement and interactivity to AI-generated art.

Example:
A static image of "a dancer in mid-leap" could be animated using AI to show the full sequence of the dance move, creating a dynamic piece that captures the fluidity of motion.

5. Enhanced Text-to-Image Synthesis

Technology:
Text-to-image synthesis is becoming more precise and detailed, allowing for the generation of complex scenes with high fidelity from even more abstract and detailed prompts.

Example:
A writer could describe a scene like "a bustling marketplace in an ancient city at sunset, with merchants selling exotic goods, children playing, and a musician performing on a street corner." The AI would generate a richly detailed and accurate image based on this description.

Practical Examples of Future Trends and Technologies

Example 1: AR and VR Integration *Scenario:* Creating an interactive art exhibit. *Future Process:* Use AI to generate detailed scenes for a virtual reality art exhibit. Visitors wearing VR headsets can explore different environments, such as "a coral reef teeming with marine life" and "a futuristic cityscape," interacting with elements in real-time and experiencing the art in an immersive, multisensory way.

Example 2: Real-Time Collaboration *Scenario:* Designing a new video game world. *Future Process:* A team of artists and designers use a real-time collaboration tool to create the game's environments. One team member generates the prompt "an enchanted forest with magical creatures and hidden ruins," while others refine and add details like "glowing pathways" and "ancient statues covered in moss," all while seeing each other's contributions live.

Example 3: Personalized AI Models *Scenario:* Creating a unique series of artworks. *Future Process:* An artist trains a personalized AI model on their specific style, characterized by "bold colors and geometric patterns." They then input prompts like "a bustling city at night" and "a serene mountain lake at dawn," with the AI generating images that maintain their distinctive aesthetic while incorporating the described scenes.

Example 4: Ethical AI Use *Scenario:* Developing a marketing campaign. *Future Process:* A company uses an AI tool designed to ensure ethical representation in its promotional materials. When generating images for a campaign on workplace diversity, the AI produces scenes like "a diverse team of professionals collaborating in an office" and "a mentor guiding a young apprentice," ensuring inclusive and respectful depictions.

Example 5: Automated Animation *Scenario:* Producing an animated short film. *Future Process:* An animator uses AI tools to generate key frames based on prompts like "a hero battling a dragon in a stormy landscape." The AI not only creates the static images but also animates the scenes, adding dynamic movement and special effects like "lightning flashing in the background" and "the dragon's fiery breath."

Best Practices for Embracing Emerging Trends and Technologies

1. Stay Informed and Adaptive

Practice:
Keep up with the latest advancements in AI technology and be willing to adapt your creative processes to incorporate new tools and techniques.

Example:
Regularly read industry publications, attend tech conferences, and participate in webinars to stay informed about new developments and how they can enhance your work.

2. Experiment and Innovate

Practice:

Experiment with new AI tools and techniques to discover unique applications and push the boundaries of your creativity.

Example:

Test different AI tools for various aspects of your projects, such as using GANs for generating realistic textures or neural style transfer for blending artistic styles, to find innovative solutions that enhance your art.

3. Prioritize Ethics and Inclusivity

Practice:

Ensure that your use of AI tools respects ethical guidelines and promotes inclusivity. Regularly review your work to avoid biases and stereotypes.

Example:

Before finalizing any AI-generated project, conduct a thorough review to ensure it represents diverse groups fairly and respectfully, making adjustments as needed to uphold ethical standards.

4. Collaborate and Share Knowledge

Practice:

Collaborate with other artists, developers, and AI experts to share knowledge and learn from each other's experiences.

Example:

Join online forums and local meetups focused on AI art, where you can discuss challenges, share successes, and collaborate on projects that leverage emerging technologies.

5. Embrace Multidisciplinary Approaches

Practice:

Combine AI-generated art with other disciplines, such as sound design, interactive media, and traditional art forms, to create richer, more immersive experiences.

Example:
Work with musicians and sound designers to create an interactive installation where AI-generated visuals are paired with dynamic soundscapes that react to viewer movements and environmental factors.

The future of AI art and prompt writing is bright, driven by emerging trends and technologies that expand creative possibilities and streamline the artistic process. Enhanced language models, AR and VR integration, real-time collaboration tools, AI-enhanced creativity assistants, personalized AI models, and ethical AI development are set to transform the landscape of digital art. By staying informed, experimenting with new tools, prioritizing ethics and inclusivity, collaborating with others, and embracing multidisciplinary approaches, artists and creators can harness these advancements to produce innovative, impactful, and responsible AI-generated art. This future promises a dynamic and inclusive evolution of the creative process, where technology and artistry intersect to push the boundaries of what is possible.

Predictions For Future Developments

The future of AI art and prompt writing is poised for remarkable advancements driven by continuous innovation in technology, creative practices, and interdisciplinary collaboration. As AI systems become more sophisticated and integrated into various artistic workflows, several key developments are predicted to shape the landscape of AI-generated art.

Predictions for Future Developments

1. Hyper-Realistic Image Generation

Prediction:

AI models will advance to create hyper-realistic images indistinguishable from photographs, enabling artists to produce highly detailed and lifelike scenes.

Example:

Artists will use AI to generate hyper-realistic portraits based on prompts like "an elderly man with deep wrinkles, wearing a fedora, with a background of a bustling city street at dusk." The resulting image would capture intricate facial details, realistic lighting, and environmental textures, making it virtually indistinguishable from a real photograph.

2. Enhanced Contextual Understanding

Prediction:

Future AI models will possess a deeper understanding of context, allowing for more nuanced and contextually appropriate art generation based on complex prompts.

Example:

A prompt such as "a romantic dinner in a quaint Parisian bistro, with soft jazz playing in the background and candlelight illuminating the table" will result in an image that accurately captures the ambiance, including details like the style of the bistro, the warm glow of the candles, and subtle elements that convey the romantic setting.

3. Real-Time Interactive Art Creation

Prediction:

AI will enable real-time interactive art creation, where users can manipulate and adjust art pieces dynamically, creating a highly engaging and personalized experience.

Example:

Using a tablet or VR headset, an artist can interactively adjust elements of an AI-generated landscape, such as changing the time of day, altering the weather, or adding characters and objects. This interactivity will allow for immediate feedback and on-the-fly creativity, enhancing the creative process.

4. Cross-Disciplinary Integration

Prediction:
AI-generated art will increasingly integrate with other disciplines such as literature, music, and film, leading to more holistic and immersive creative projects.

Example:
A collaborative project might involve AI-generated visuals paired with AI-composed music and AI-written narrative, creating a multimedia experience where each element complements and enhances the others. For instance, an interactive storybook app could feature AI-generated illustrations that change based on the AI-generated music score and the user's interactions with the text.

5. Personalized and Adaptive AI Models

Prediction:
AI models will become more personalized and adaptive, learning from individual artists' styles and preferences to assist in creating highly customized and unique artworks.

Example:
An artist specializing in surrealism could train an AI model on their past works. When provided with a prompt like "a dreamlike landscape with floating islands and waterfalls cascading into the sky," the AI generates images that closely align with the artist's distinctive style, incorporating their preferred color palettes, textures, and compositional techniques.

6. Ethical and Inclusive AI Art Practices

Prediction:

There will be a significant emphasis on developing AI art practices that are ethical and inclusive, ensuring fair representation and avoiding biases in AI-generated content.

Example:

AI tools will be designed with built-in checks to prevent the generation of biased or stereotypical images. For a prompt like "a team of scientists working in a lab," the AI will ensure diverse representation, showing scientists of different genders, ethnicities, and abilities working together, reflecting real-world diversity and inclusion.

7. AI-Driven Collaborative Platforms

Prediction:

Collaborative platforms powered by AI will enable artists from around the world to work together seamlessly on large-scale projects, sharing resources and ideas in real-time.

Example:

An online platform could host a global art project where artists contribute AI-generated pieces to a collective mural. The AI facilitates collaboration by harmonizing different styles and ensuring a coherent final piece, while also suggesting improvements and new ideas based on the contributions.

8. Evolution of AI Art Marketplaces

Prediction:

AI-generated art will see the development of dedicated marketplaces where artists can sell and trade AI-created works, expanding the commercial potential of AI art.

Example:

A digital marketplace specifically for AI-generated art will allow artists to list their creations for sale, with AI tools assisting in setting prices based on factors like complexity, uniqueness, and market trends. Collectors can purchase unique AI-generated pieces, knowing they are supporting a blend of human creativity and machine innovation.

Practical Examples of Future Developments

Example 1: Hyper-Realistic Portraits *Scenario:* Creating a family portrait with AI. *Future Process:* An artist inputs a prompt like "a family of four posing in their living room, with a large window showing a garden outside." The AI generates a hyper-realistic image capturing each family member's features, the room's decor, and the garden's details with photographic accuracy.

Example 2: Interactive Digital Exhibits *Scenario:* Designing an interactive museum exhibit. *Future Process:* Visitors use VR headsets to explore AI-generated environments based on historical events. A prompt like "ancient Rome at the height of its power" results in a fully immersive experience where users can walk through the streets, interact with AI-generated citizens, and learn about Roman culture dynamically.

Example 3: Multimedia Storytelling *Scenario:* Producing an interactive digital novel. *Future Process:* Writers collaborate with AI to generate illustrations and background music for a digital novel. A chapter described as "a mysterious forest at night, with eerie sounds and hidden creatures" features AI-generated visuals and an AI-composed soundtrack that adapts to the reader's pace and choices.

Example 4: Personalized Artistic Styles *Scenario:* Developing a unique art series. *Future Process:* An artist trains an AI model on their portfolio of abstract art. For a new project, they input prompts like "abstract interpretation of urban life" and receive images that reflect their personal style, incorporating familiar patterns, colors, and themes.

Example 5: Inclusive Representation *Scenario:* Creating educational materials. *Future Process:* An AI tool designed for inclusivity generates images for a textbook on modern science. Prompts like "a classroom with diverse students conducting experiments" result in images that show a wide range of ethnicities, genders, and abilities, promoting diversity in educational content.

Example 6: Global Art Collaboration *Scenario:* Building a collaborative digital mural. *Future Process:* Artists from various countries use a real-time collaborative platform to contribute AI-generated elements to a digital mural. Prompts like "elements representing cultural heritage" result in a mural that blends diverse styles and traditions, curated by AI to ensure a harmonious and integrated final artwork.

Example 7: AI Art Marketplace *Scenario:* Selling AI-generated art. *Future Process:* An artist lists their AI-generated works on a specialized marketplace. The AI helps price the artworks based on market trends and the artist's popularity. Collectors browse and purchase pieces like "a futuristic cityscape at dawn" or "a surreal underwater world," supporting the artist financially.

Best Practices for Embracing Future Developments

1. Embrace Continuous Learning

Practice:
Stay updated with the latest technological advancements and artistic trends to leverage new tools and techniques effectively.

Example:
Regularly participate in online courses, webinars, and workshops focused on AI art and digital creativity to keep your skills current and innovative.

2. Foster Ethical Use

Practice:
Prioritize ethical considerations in your AI art practice, ensuring inclusivity, fairness, and respect for intellectual property.

Example:
Before releasing AI-generated artwork, review it for potential biases and ensure it represents diverse groups fairly. Respect copyright laws by avoiding the use of protected materials without permission.

3. Encourage Collaboration

Practice:
Engage in collaborative projects that bring together diverse talents and perspectives, enhancing the richness and creativity of AI-generated art.

Example:
Join interdisciplinary teams, including AI developers, artists, musicians, and writers, to create multimedia projects that push the boundaries of traditional art forms.

4. Innovate and Experiment

Practice:
Continuously experiment with new AI tools and creative techniques to discover unique applications and expand your artistic horizons.

Example:
Use AI to generate initial concepts and explore different artistic styles, combining them with traditional techniques to create hybrid artworks that stand out.

5. Advocate for Responsible AI Development

Practice:
Support and advocate for the development of AI technologies that prioritize ethical considerations and inclusivity.

Example:
Participate in discussions and initiatives that promote responsible AI development, ensuring that new tools and models are designed with fairness and ethical use in mind.

The future of AI art and prompt writing is set to be transformative, with advancements leading to hyper-realistic image generation, enhanced contextual understanding, real-time interactive creation, cross-disciplinary integration, personalized AI models, ethical and inclusive practices, AI-driven collaborative platforms, and the evolution of AI art marketplaces. By embracing continuous learning, fostering ethical use, encouraging collaboration, innovating, and advocating for responsible AI development, artists and creators can harness these future developments to produce innovative, impactful, and responsible AI-generated art. This dynamic future promises to expand the creative possibilities and redefine the intersection of technology and artistry.

The Evolving Role of Prompt Writers

As AI art generation technologies continue to advance, the role of prompt writers is evolving in exciting and multifaceted ways. Prompt writers play a crucial part in bridging the gap between human creativity and machine capability, crafting detailed and imaginative prompts that guide AI systems to produce high-quality, meaningful art.

The Evolving Role of Prompt Writers

1. Creative Directors of AI Art

Evolution:
Prompt writers are becoming the creative directors of AI-generated art, orchestrating the elements of a scene or concept through meticulously crafted prompts.

Example:
A prompt writer might direct an AI to create a scene of "a bustling medieval marketplace at dawn, with vendors setting up stalls, children playing, and knights in shining armor riding through the town square." This involves specifying not only the visual elements but also the mood, lighting, and interactions within the scene.

2. Curators of AI Content

Evolution:
Prompt writers are increasingly acting as curators, selecting and refining the best outputs from AI-generated content to ensure the highest quality and coherence.

Example:
After generating multiple versions of "a futuristic cityscape with neon lights and flying cars," the prompt writer reviews and curates the best images, refining the prompts based on feedback and iterating to improve the final selection.

3. Collaborators with AI

Evolution:
The relationship between prompt writers and AI is becoming more collaborative, with writers using AI suggestions and real-time feedback to refine and enhance their prompts.

Example:
A prompt writer starts with a basic idea, such as "a serene forest glade," and uses an AI tool that suggests additions like "a gentle stream flowing through, with deer grazing by the water." The

writer integrates these suggestions, creating a richer, more detailed scene.

4. Specialists in Ethical AI Use

Evolution:
Prompt writers are taking on the role of ensuring ethical and unbiased AI content creation, developing prompts that promote inclusivity and diversity.

Example:
When tasked with generating images for a health campaign, a prompt writer carefully crafts prompts that represent people of various ages, ethnicities, and abilities, such as "a diverse group of doctors and nurses working together in a modern hospital setting."

5. Innovators of Multimodal Art

Evolution:
Prompt writers are expanding their skills to include multimodal prompts that integrate text, visuals, and audio, creating immersive and interactive art experiences.

Example:
A prompt writer might create a comprehensive prompt for an interactive exhibit: "a virtual reality tour of an ancient Roman city, with background sounds of a bustling marketplace, music from street performers, and detailed descriptions of daily life appearing as users explore different areas."

6. Educators and Advocates for AI Art

Evolution:
Prompt writers are becoming educators and advocates, sharing their expertise and promoting the understanding and appreciation of AI art.

Example:
An experienced prompt writer might conduct workshops and seminars, teaching others how to craft effective prompts and demonstrating the potential of AI in art creation. They may also write articles or create online tutorials to share best practices and innovative techniques.

Practical Examples of Evolving Responsibilities

Example 1: Creative Directing *Scenario:* Crafting a scene for a digital painting. *Process:* The prompt writer designs a prompt like "a tranquil Japanese garden at sunset, with cherry blossoms falling gently, a stone lantern by a koi pond, and a tea ceremony taking place in a traditional gazebo." They guide the AI to focus on the specific elements and the overall ambiance of serenity and tradition.

Example 2: Curating AI Content *Scenario:* Developing a series of book covers. *Process:* The prompt writer generates multiple variations of "a mysterious forest with a hidden path leading to an ancient castle." They curate the best images, considering factors like composition, mood, and detail, and provide refined prompts to achieve the desired aesthetic for each cover.

Example 3: Collaborating with AI *Scenario:* Designing an animated short film. *Process:* Starting with a concept like "a whimsical underwater adventure," the prompt writer collaborates with AI to generate scenes and character designs. The AI suggests additions such as "bioluminescent plants and colorful coral reefs," which the writer incorporates to enhance the visual narrative.

Example 4: Ensuring Ethical AI Use *Scenario:* Creating educational materials for schools. *Process:* The prompt writer develops inclusive prompts like "a classroom with students of different backgrounds working together on a science project," ensuring fair representation and avoiding stereotypes. They review

AI outputs to ensure accuracy and inclusivity before finalizing the images.

Example 5: Innovating Multimodal Art *Scenario:* Producing an immersive multimedia installation. *Process:* The prompt writer creates a multimodal prompt for an installation: "an enchanted forest that changes with the seasons, with ambient sounds of wildlife and dynamic lighting effects that shift from dawn to dusk." They integrate text descriptions, visual elements, and audio to create a cohesive and engaging experience.

Example 6: Educating and Advocating *Scenario:* Leading a workshop on AI art. *Process:* The prompt writer organizes a workshop titled "Unlocking Creativity with AI," where they demonstrate how to craft effective prompts and showcase examples of AI-generated art. They provide hands-on exercises, allowing participants to practice and develop their prompt-writing skills.

Best Practices for Evolving as a Prompt Writer

1. Embrace Continuous Learning

Practice:
Stay informed about the latest developments in AI technology, art trends, and ethical guidelines. Regularly update your skills and knowledge to remain at the forefront of the field.

Example:
Enroll in online courses, attend industry conferences, and participate in AI art communities to keep your skills sharp and your understanding of new technologies current.

2. Foster Collaboration and Feedback

Practice:
Engage with other artists, AI developers, and prompt writers to

exchange ideas, share feedback, and collaborate on projects. Collaboration enhances creativity and innovation.

Example:
Join online forums and local art groups to discuss your work, seek constructive criticism, and collaborate on joint projects that blend different skills and perspectives.

3. Prioritize Ethical and Inclusive Practices

Practice:
Ensure that your prompts and the resulting AI-generated art are ethical and inclusive, promoting diversity and avoiding biases.

Example:
Review all AI outputs for fairness and representation, and be mindful of cultural sensitivities when crafting prompts. Aim to create art that reflects a wide range of human experiences and perspectives.

4. Experiment and Innovate

Practice:
Regularly experiment with new techniques, tools, and ideas to push the boundaries of what is possible with AI-generated art. Innovation keeps your work fresh and exciting.

Example:
Try combining AI-generated visuals with other art forms, such as integrating poetry or music into your projects, to create unique and immersive art experiences.

5. Educate and Advocate

Practice:
Share your knowledge and passion for AI art with others. Educate aspiring artists and the public about the potential and ethical considerations of AI in art.

Example:
Conduct workshops, write articles, and create online tutorials that demystify AI art and provide practical guidance on crafting effective prompts and using AI tools responsibly.

The role of prompt writers in AI art is evolving into one of greater creativity, collaboration, and responsibility. As creative directors, curators, collaborators, ethical guardians, innovators, and educators, prompt writers are at the forefront of the integration of AI into the artistic process. By embracing continuous learning, fostering collaboration, prioritizing ethics, experimenting with new ideas, and sharing their expertise, prompt writers can harness the full potential of AI technologies to create impactful, inclusive, and innovative art. This evolving role not only enhances the quality and diversity of AI-generated art but also ensures that the creative possibilities of AI are explored responsibly and ethically.

Conclusion

The future of AI art and prompt writing holds immense potential for technological advancements, evolving creative practices, and addressing ethical considerations. Improved AI models, real-time feedback, multimodal capabilities, collaborative creation, personalized art, and interactive experiences will shape the next era of digital art. By embracing continuous learning, experimentation, ethical responsibility, collaborative approaches, and personalization, artists and developers can harness the full potential of AI tools like DALL·E 3.0 to create innovative and impactful art. This future promises to expand the boundaries of creativity while ensuring that AI-generated art remains responsible, inclusive, and respectful of intellectual property and cultural diversity.

Example Prompts and Images

Prompt: "A tranquil Japanese garden at sunset, with cherry blossoms falling gently, a stone lantern by a koi pond, and a tea ceremony taking place in a traditional gazebo."

Prompt: "A futuristic cityscape with neon lights and flying cars, reflecting in the wet streets during a rainy night."

Prompt: "A serene forest glade, with a gentle stream flowing through, deer grazing by the water, and sunlight filtering through the trees."

Prompt: "A diverse group of doctors and nurses working together in a modern hospital setting, showcasing inclusivity and teamwork."

Prompt: "A virtual reality tour of an ancient Roman city, with background sounds of a bustling marketplace, music from street performers, and detailed descriptions of daily life appearing as users explore different areas."

Prompt: "An interactive workshop where artists are learning to craft effective AI prompts, with screens showing various AI-generated images and participants discussing their ideas."

Complex Prompts and Images

Fantasy Landscape:

"A mystical forest illuminated by bioluminescent plants, with towering ancient trees draped in vines. In the center, a sparkling waterfall cascades into a crystal-clear pond surrounded by luminescent mushrooms and glowing flowers. Ethereal creatures like fairies and wisps float around, casting a magical glow. The sky above is twilight, with stars beginning to appear, and a full moon casting a soft, silver light through the tree canopy."

Steampunk City:

"A bustling steampunk city at dusk, with towering buildings made of brick and metal, adorned with intricate gears and steam-powered machinery. The streets are lined with cobblestone and illuminated by gas lanterns. Airships float in the sky, tethered to tall spires. People dressed in Victorian-era clothing, with goggles and mechanical accessories, walk the streets. A grand clock tower stands in the background, its gears visibly turning, and steam rises from various chimneys and street vendors."

Futuristic Sci-Fi Scene:

"A sprawling futuristic cityscape at night, filled with towering skyscrapers made of glass and metal, illuminated by neon lights and holographic advertisements. Flying cars zoom between buildings, while pedestrians walk on elevated walkways. The skyline is dominated by a massive space elevator reaching into the sky, connecting to a space station visible in orbit. Below, a bustling marketplace with robotic vendors and diverse alien species interacting. The sky is filled with stars and distant planets, with a large, glowing moon casting a bluish light over the city."

Historical Battle Scene:

"A detailed depiction of an ancient Roman battlefield, with legions of Roman soldiers in full armor clashing with barbarian tribes. The scene is chaotic, with soldiers wielding swords and shields, archers launching arrows, and cavalry charging. In the background, the Roman standard bearers hold high their banners, while commanders on horseback shout orders. The battlefield is littered with fallen warriors, broken weapons, and makeshift barricades. Dust and smoke fill the air, creating a sense of intensity and struggle."

Magical Underwater Kingdom:

"An enchanting underwater kingdom, with grand coral palaces and shimmering seaweed gardens. Mermaids and mermen swim gracefully, adorned with pearls and shells. Schools of colorful fish dart through the water, while majestic sea creatures like turtles and dolphins glide by. The seabed is covered in vibrant corals and mysterious shipwrecks. Bioluminescent plants provide a soft glow, illuminating the scene. In the distance, a grand throne made of coral and seashells stands in the center of the kingdom, with a regal mermaid queen seated upon it."

Cyberpunk Alleyway:

"A dark, narrow cyberpunk alleyway in a dystopian city, illuminated by flickering neon signs in various languages. The walls are covered in graffiti and posters, with cables and pipes running along them. Trash and debris litter the ground, and steam rises from manholes. Street vendors sell cybernetic enhancements and black-market goods from makeshift stalls. People with cybernetic implants and glowing tattoos pass by, some engaged in shady dealings. In the background, towering skyscrapers with bright holographic advertisements loom over the alley, casting a vibrant yet oppressive light."

Victorian-Era Haunted Mansion:

"A grand, eerie Victorian-era mansion on a foggy night, with towering spires and intricate Gothic architecture. The mansion is surrounded by overgrown gardens and a wrought-iron fence. Windows are dark, with a few flickering candlelights visible inside. A large, ornate front door creaks open, revealing a dimly lit interior with antique furniture covered in dust and cobwebs. Ghostly figures and shadows move through the hallways, and a grand staircase leads to the upper floors. Outside, the full moon casts an eerie glow over the scene, and a howling wind adds to the sense of foreboding."

Post-Apocalyptic Desert:

"A vast post-apocalyptic desert landscape under a burning orange sky, with remnants of a once-thriving city now reduced to ruins. Rusted, skeletal frames of skyscrapers stand amid the sand dunes, and abandoned vehicles half-buried in sand litter the area. Scavengers in makeshift armor made from scrap metal roam the wasteland, while a lone figure in a tattered cloak rides a mutated beast. In the background, a crumbling billboard displays faded advertisements from the past. The scene is bathed in an eerie glow, with dust storms visible on the horizon."

Enchanted Medieval Library:

"An enormous medieval library with towering bookshelves that reach the vaulted ceiling, filled with ancient tomes and scrolls. Intricate stained-glass windows cast colorful light across the room, illuminating floating candles and enchanted quills that write on their own. A spiral staircase made of wrought iron winds up to a balcony overlooking the main floor. Wizards and scholars in long robes peruse the collection, and a magical portal glows softly in one corner, guarded by a stone gargoyle. The air is thick with the smell of old parchment and the hum of magical energy."

Futuristic Underwater Research Facility:

"A sprawling underwater research facility made of sleek glass and steel, located on the ocean floor. The facility is illuminated by bright artificial lights and surrounded by vibrant coral reefs and diverse marine life. Scientists in advanced diving suits and robotic drones move through transparent tunnels that connect different sections of the facility. A massive central dome houses a cutting-edge laboratory, where holographic screens display data and 3D models. Outside, a giant observation window offers a breathtaking view of a nearby underwater volcano, with schools of fish and bioluminescent creatures swimming past."

Haunted Carnival:

"A decrepit, haunted carnival at midnight, with rusting rides and faded, tattered tents. The Ferris wheel stands eerily still, its carriages creaking in the wind, while the carousel's broken horses seem to move on their own. Fog rolls through the carnival grounds, obscuring twisted clown faces and sinister funhouse mirrors. Ghostly figures and shadowy apparitions move between the attractions, and a creepy, out-of-tune calliope plays haunting melodies. The moon casts a ghostly light over the scene, and the distant sound of a child's laughter echoes through the empty grounds."

Space Colony on a Distant Planet:

"A bustling space colony on a distant, alien planet, with futuristic buildings made of sleek metal and glass. The colony is set within a large crater, with a protective dome overhead shielding it from the planet's harsh atmosphere. Colonists in advanced space suits move through the streets, alongside alien creatures and robots. In the center of the colony, a towering structure serves as the main hub, with spacecraft landing and taking off from a nearby pad. The alien landscape outside the dome features towering rock formations, strange plant life, and a distant, ringed planet visible in the sky."

Dr. Hesham Mohamed Elsherif

Victorian-Era Steampunk Laboratory:

"A cluttered Victorian-era steampunk laboratory filled with a mix of antique furniture and advanced machinery powered by steam and clockwork. Brass gears and cogs turn in intricate mechanisms, and pipes run along the walls, emitting occasional puffs of steam. The room is dimly lit by gas lamps and the glow of strange, alchemical experiments bubbling away in glass beakers. An eccentric inventor in a waistcoat and goggles works at a cluttered workbench, surrounded by blueprints, tools, and mechanical gadgets. A large window offers a view of a smog-filled cityscape with towering smokestacks and airships flying by."

Ancient Mythological Battlefield:

"A grand, mythological battlefield where gods, demigods, and mythical creatures clash in an epic struggle. The landscape is marked by jagged mountains and stormy skies, with lightning illuminating the scene. On one side, a group of armored warriors led by a powerful deity wielding a glowing weapon charge into battle. On the other, monstrous creatures like dragons, minotaurs, and giants roar and fight back. The ground is littered with fallen warriors and broken weapons, and a river of lava flows through the center of the battlefield. Divine energy and magical spells light up the chaotic scene."

APPENDICES

Glossary Of Terms

A comprehensive glossary of terms is essential for understanding the complex and specialized language often used in AI art and prompt writing. This section provides definitions and examples for key terms, helping readers navigate the technical vocabulary and concepts involved in AI-generated art.

Artificial Intelligence (AI)

Definition: A branch of computer science focused on creating systems capable of performing tasks that typically require human intelligence, such as visual perception, speech recognition, decision-making, and language translation.

Example: DALL·E 3.0 is an AI model that generates images from textual descriptions.

Prompt Writing

Definition: The process of crafting detailed and specific textual descriptions that guide AI models in generating desired outputs, such as images, text, or other media.

Example: Writing a prompt like "A tranquil Japanese garden at sunset, with cherry blossoms falling gently, a stone lantern by a koi pond, and a tea ceremony taking place in a traditional gazebo" for an AI model to create a corresponding image.

Generative Adversarial Networks (GANs)

Definition: A class of AI algorithms used in unsupervised learning that consists of two neural networks, a generator and a discriminator, which work together to create realistic synthetic data.

Example: GANs are often used to generate high-quality images that can be difficult to distinguish from real photographs.

Deep Learning

Definition: A subset of machine learning involving neural networks with many layers (deep neural networks) that can learn and make intelligent decisions on their own by processing large amounts of data.

Example: Deep learning techniques are used to train AI models like DALL·E 3.0 to understand and generate complex images from text descriptions.

Neural Network

Definition: A computational model inspired by the human brain's network of neurons, used in machine learning to recognize patterns and solve various tasks.

Example: Neural networks are the backbone of AI systems, enabling them to learn from data and improve their performance over time.

Training Data

Definition: A set of data used to teach AI models to recognize patterns and make decisions. The quality and quantity of training data significantly impact the model's accuracy and effectiveness.

Example: An AI model trained to generate art might use thousands of images and their descriptions as training data to learn how to create new, similar images.

Bias in AI
Definition: A systematic error that occurs in AI models when they make prejudiced decisions based on biased training data, often leading to unfair or discriminatory outcomes.
Example: If an AI model is trained primarily on images of people from a single ethnic group, it may perform poorly in recognizing or generating images of people from other ethnic groups.

Augmented Reality (AR)
Definition: A technology that overlays digital information, such as images, sounds, or other data, onto the real-world environment, typically through a smartphone or AR glasses.
Example: Using AR, a user can view a digitally generated model of a historical artifact placed in their real-world living room.

Virtual Reality (VR)
Definition: A fully immersive digital environment that simulates a real or imagined world, experienced through VR headsets and other sensory devices.
Example: In VR, users can explore an AI-generated Roman city, walking through streets and interacting with virtual citizens as if they were actually there.

Ethical AI
Definition: The practice of developing and using AI in ways that are fair, transparent, and respectful of human rights, ensuring that AI benefits all of society without causing harm.
Example: Ensuring that an AI model used in healthcare does not favor one demographic over another in diagnosing and treating patients.

Multimodal AI

Definition: AI systems that can process and generate multiple types of data, such as text, images, and audio, to create richer and more integrated outputs.

Example: An AI model that can generate a video with both visual and audio elements based on a textual description, such as "a bustling marketplace with the sound of vendors shouting and background music playing."

Natural Language Processing (NLP)

Definition: A field of AI that focuses on the interaction between computers and humans through natural language, enabling computers to understand, interpret, and respond to human language.

Example: NLP is used in virtual assistants like Siri and Alexa to understand and respond to user commands and questions.

Overfitting

Definition: A modeling error that occurs when an AI model learns the training data too well, including noise and outliers, resulting in poor performance on new, unseen data.

Example: An AI model trained to generate art that perfectly replicates its training images but fails to create original and varied new artworks.

Supervised Learning

Definition: A type of machine learning where the model is trained on labeled data, meaning each training example is paired with an output label. The model learns to map inputs to outputs based on this data.

Example: Training an AI to recognize images of cats by providing a large dataset of cat images labeled as "cat."

Unsupervised Learning

Definition: A type of machine learning where the model is trained on data without labeled responses, identifying patterns and relationships within the data on its own.

Example: An AI model clustering similar artworks together without being told what each artwork represents.

Zero-Shot Learning

Definition: A learning model that can correctly make predictions on new, unseen classes or categories without any prior training data for those specific classes.

Example: An AI model generating a convincing image of a "blue apple" even though it has never been trained on images of blue apples specifically.

Latent Space

Definition: A representation of compressed data in a lower-dimensional space that captures the essential features needed to generate new data points.

Example: In GANs, the latent space helps in generating new images by interpolating between known images in this compressed form.

Sample Prompts and Outputs

Providing sample prompts and their corresponding AI-generated outputs is an essential part of understanding how to craft effective prompts for AI art generation. This section offers a variety of prompts across different themes and styles, along with descriptions of the resulting outputs, illustrating the range and capabilities of AI art models.

Sample Prompt 1: Fantasy Landscape

Prompt:
"A mystical forest with towering ancient trees, bioluminescent plants, and a glowing waterfall cascading into a crystal-clear pool. Elven archers patrol the area, and a unicorn drinks from the pool under a moonlit sky."

Output Description:
The generated image depicts a lush, verdant forest with massive trees whose leaves emit a soft, green glow. The waterfall, illuminated by bioluminescence, adds a magical light to the scene. Elven archers, dressed in intricate armor, are seen perched in the trees and on the ground, maintaining vigilant watch. A unicorn with a shimmering coat is gracefully drinking from the pool, reflecting the light of a full moon overhead.

Sample Prompt 2: Futuristic Cityscape

Prompt:
"A bustling futuristic city at night, filled with neon signs, hovering vehicles, and skyscrapers adorned with digital billboards. People in sleek, modern attire walk the streets, and robots assist with everyday tasks."

Output Description:
The output shows a vibrant cityscape illuminated by neon lights in various colors, casting a glow on the reflective surfaces of the buildings and streets. Hovering vehicles zoom through the air between towering skyscrapers that display large digital advertisements. The streets are crowded with people wearing stylish, futuristic clothing, while robots in different shapes and sizes are seen helping with chores like carrying groceries and directing traffic.

Sample Prompt 3: Historical Scene

Prompt:
"A bustling marketplace in ancient Rome, with vendors selling spices, fruits, and fabrics. Citizens in traditional Roman attire barter and converse, while a legionnaire stands guard near a marble fountain."

Output Description:
The generated image captures the lively atmosphere of an ancient Roman marketplace. Stalls overflowing with colorful spices, fresh fruits, and rich fabrics line the streets. Roman citizens, dressed in togas and tunics, are engaged in animated conversations and bartering with vendors. A legionnaire in full armor stands vigilantly by a beautifully crafted marble fountain, which serves as a central gathering point in the market.

Sample Prompt 4: Surreal Artwork

Prompt:
"A dreamlike scene featuring floating islands connected by wooden bridges, with waterfalls cascading into the clouds below.

Strange, whimsical creatures inhabit the islands, and the sky is filled with swirling, colorful nebulae."

Output Description:

The output presents a surreal and fantastical landscape where multiple floating islands are suspended in the sky, interconnected by rickety wooden bridges. Each island has its unique ecosystem, inhabited by whimsical creatures resembling a mix of real and mythical animals. Waterfalls pour from the edges of the islands, disappearing into the dense, fluffy clouds below. The sky above is a canvas of swirling colors, resembling nebulae, adding to the dreamlike quality of the scene.

Sample Prompt 5: Modern Interior Design

Prompt:

"A sleek, modern living room with minimalist furniture, large floor-to-ceiling windows offering a city skyline view, and a sophisticated color palette of whites, grays, and blacks. A cozy fireplace is set into a marble wall."

Output Description:

The generated image showcases a stylish, contemporary living room. The furniture is minimalist, with clean lines and a monochromatic color scheme dominated by whites, grays, and blacks. Large floor-to-ceiling windows provide a breathtaking view of the city skyline, filling the room with natural light. A modern fireplace, set into a sleek marble wall, adds a touch of warmth and elegance to the space. The overall ambiance is one of sophistication and comfort.

Sample Prompt 6: Underwater Scene

Prompt:
"An underwater kingdom with colorful coral reefs, ancient sunken ruins, and schools of exotic fish swimming through crystal-clear water. Mermaids play and explore the ruins, while a giant sea turtle glides gracefully overhead."

Output Description:
The output reveals a vibrant underwater world teeming with life. Brightly colored coral reefs form the backdrop, interspersed with the ancient ruins of a once-great civilization, now covered in marine growth. Schools of exotic fish dart among the coral, adding flashes of color. Mermaids with shimmering tails are depicted playing and exploring the ruins, their movements graceful and fluid. A majestic sea turtle is seen gliding above, casting a shadow over the scene as it swims effortlessly through the water.

Sample Prompt 7: Steampunk Invention

Prompt:
"A detailed illustration of a steampunk-inspired airship, with brass gears, leather sails, and intricate clockwork mechanisms. The ship hovers above a Victorian cityscape, with inventors and engineers working on the deck."

Output Description:
The image showcases a beautifully detailed steampunk airship, featuring a combination of brass and copper elements, leather sails, and visible clockwork gears. The airship hovers majestically above a Victorian-era city, with smokestacks and cobblestone streets below. On the deck of the airship, inventors and engineers dressed in Victorian attire are busy adjusting the machinery and overseeing the ship's operations. The scene captures the essence of steampunk aesthetics, blending historical elements with fantastical technology.

Sample Prompt 8: Fantasy Character Portrait

Prompt:

"A portrait of a fierce warrior queen, with long flowing hair, wearing ornate armor adorned with gemstones. She holds a glowing sword, and her piercing eyes reflect determination and strength."

Output Description:

The generated portrait features a powerful and regal warrior queen. Her long, flowing hair frames her face, which is marked by a determined and intense expression. She is dressed in elaborate armor that glistens with embedded gemstones, each piece crafted with intricate detail. In her hand, she holds a glowing sword that emanates a soft light, adding to her commanding presence. Her eyes, filled with resolve, draw the viewer in, conveying her strength and leadership.

Sample Prompt 9: Sci-Fi Laboratory

Prompt:

"A high-tech laboratory filled with futuristic gadgets, holographic displays, and robotic assistants. Scientists in sleek lab coats are conducting experiments, and a central computer console glows with complex data visualizations."

Output Description:

The output depicts a cutting-edge science fiction laboratory brimming with advanced technology. Futuristic gadgets and devices are spread across workstations, while holographic displays project various data and schematics into the air. Robotic assistants move efficiently around the lab, aiding the scientists. The scientists, dressed in sleek, modern lab coats, are deeply engrossed in their experiments. At the center of the lab, a large computer console glows with intricate data visualizations, highlighting the lab's sophisticated capabilities.

Sample Prompt 10: Cozy Reading Nook

Prompt:
"A cozy reading nook with a large, cushioned window seat, surrounded by shelves filled with books. Soft, warm lighting creates a relaxing atmosphere, and a cup of steaming tea sits on a small side table."

Output Description:
The generated image presents a charming and inviting reading nook. A spacious, cushioned window seat beckons with an array of plush pillows, perfect for curling up with a book. Bookshelves packed with a variety of books surround the nook, creating a literary sanctuary. The warm, ambient lighting enhances the cozy atmosphere, casting a gentle glow over the space. A small side table holds a cup of steaming tea, completing the scene and inviting the viewer to settle in and relax with a good read.

Additional Resources and References

A comprehensive list of additional resources and references is essential for furthering understanding and expanding knowledge in the field of AI-generated art and prompt writing.

Books

1. "The Artist's Guide to GIMP: Creative Techniques for Photographers, Artists, and Designers" Description: This book offers detailed instructions and creative techniques for using GIMP, a powerful open-source image editing software. It covers everything from basic photo retouching to advanced artistic effects. **Example:** An artist learning to refine AI-generated images can use this book to enhance their skills in color correction, layering, and texture application.

2. "Deep Learning with Python" Description: This book introduces the concepts of deep learning using Python, providing practical examples and exercises to help readers understand and implement neural networks. **Example:** An AI developer can use this book to gain insights into the algorithms behind AI models, allowing them to create custom modifications and improvements.

3. "Artificial Intelligence: A Guide for Thinking Humans" Description: A comprehensive overview of AI, its development, and its impact on various fields, including art. The book provides a balanced perspective on the capabilities and limitations of AI. **Example:** Readers can gain a foundational understanding of AI, helping them to appreciate the technology behind AI-generated art and its broader implications.

Online Courses

1. "Introduction to AI for Artists" Description: An online course designed to teach artists the basics of AI and how to use AI tools to create art. The course includes practical exercises and real-world examples. **Example:** Artists new to AI can learn how to craft effective prompts and use AI tools like DALL·E to generate creative works.

2. "Mastering Digital Art with Photoshop" Description: A series of tutorials covering advanced Photoshop techniques for digital artists. The course focuses on enhancing and refining digital art, including AI-generated images. **Example:** An artist can learn advanced editing techniques such as blending modes, layer masks, and digital painting to improve the quality of their AI-generated art.

3. "Deep Learning Specialization" Description: A comprehensive online course covering deep learning from basics to advanced topics, including neural networks, convolutional networks, and sequence models. **Example:** AI developers can deepen their understanding of deep learning, enabling them to develop more sophisticated AI models for art generation.

Software Tools

1. GIMP (GNU Image Manipulation Program) Description: A free and open-source image editor that offers a wide range of tools for photo retouching, image composition, and image authoring. **Example:** Artists can use GIMP to refine and enhance AI-generated images, applying filters, adjustments, and creative effects to achieve desired results.

2. Blender Description: An open-source 3D creation suite that supports the entirety of the 3D pipeline, including modeling, rigging, animation, simulation, rendering, compositing, and motion tracking. **Example:** Artists and developers can use Blender to create detailed 3D models and environments based on AI-generated concepts, bringing static images to life in three dimensions.

3. Adobe Photoshop Description: A powerful image editing software widely used by professionals in graphic design, photography, and digital art. **Example:** Digital artists can utilize Photoshop's extensive toolset to enhance and manipulate AI-generated images, creating polished and professional artworks.

Online Communities

1. ArtStation Description: A platform for professional artists to showcase their work, including AI-generated art. It offers portfolios, tutorials, and a marketplace. **Example:** Artists can create a profile to share their AI-generated images, receive feedback, and connect with other professionals in the field.

2. DeviantArt Description: A large online community for artists of all levels, supporting a variety of art forms, including digital art and AI-generated art. **Example:** Artists can join groups focused on AI art, participate in discussions, and receive constructive critiques to improve their work.

3. Reddit Description: A platform with numerous subreddits dedicated to different aspects of AI, digital art, and creative technologies. **Example:** Users can engage with communities like r/DigitalArt and r/AIArt to share their AI-generated creations, ask questions, and stay updated on the latest trends.

Ethical Guidelines

1. Avoiding Bias in AI Description: Guidelines and best practices for ensuring that AI-generated content is free from biases and represents diverse groups fairly. **Example:** Developers and artists can follow these guidelines to review and adjust their AI models and prompts, ensuring inclusive and respectful outputs.

2. Transparency and Disclosure Description: Recommendations for disclosing the use of AI in creating art to maintain transparency and build trust with audiences. **Example:** Artists can include statements like "This artwork was created using AI technology" in their project descriptions to inform viewers about the creative process.

3. Intellectual Property and Copyright Description: Guidelines for respecting intellectual property rights and ensuring that AI-generated art does not infringe on existing works. **Example:** Artists can seek proper permissions and give appropriate credit when using elements inspired by or derived from other works, maintaining ethical standards in their creations.

Practical Examples of Using Additional Resources

Example 1: Enhancing AI Art with GIMP *Scenario:* An artist wants to improve the lighting and color balance of an AI-generated landscape. *Process:* Using "The Artist's Guide to GIMP," the artist follows the book's tutorials to adjust the brightness, contrast, and saturation, creating a more vibrant and balanced final image.

Example 2: Learning Deep Learning with Python *Scenario:* A developer wants to customize an AI model for better art generation. *Process:* By working through "Deep Learning with Python," the developer learns how to implement and modify neural networks, allowing them to tailor an AI model to their specific artistic needs.

Example 3: Engaging with Online Communities *Scenario:* An artist seeks feedback on their latest AI-generated portrait. *Process:* The artist posts the image on ArtStation and DeviantArt, joining relevant groups and participating in discussions. They receive valuable critiques and suggestions, helping them refine their technique.

Example 4: Following Ethical Guidelines *Scenario:* A developer is creating a diverse set of character designs using AI. *Process:* By adhering to guidelines on avoiding bias in AI, the developer ensures the characters represent various ethnicities, genders, and body types accurately and respectfully.

Example 5: Taking an Online Course *Scenario:* An artist wants to learn how to integrate AI-generated elements into their digital paintings. *Process:* The artist enrolls in "Mastering Digital Art with Photoshop" and learns advanced techniques for blending AI-generated images seamlessly into their artworks.

Conclusion

This section on additional resources and references provides a valuable foundation for expanding knowledge and skills in AI-generated art and prompt writing. By utilizing books, online courses, software tools, online communities, and ethical guidelines, artists and developers can enhance their creative capabilities, stay informed about the latest trends, and ensure their work is both innovative and responsible. These resources support continuous learning and professional growth, enabling the creation of high-quality, impactful AI-generated art.